iPad in One Hour FOR LAWYERS

BY TOM MIGHELL

ABA **LawPracticeManagementSection**
MARKETING • MANAGEMENT • TECHNOLOGY • FINANCE

Commitment to Quality: The Law Practice Management Section is committed to quality in our publications. Our authors are experienced practitioners in their fields. Prior to publication, the contents of all our books are rigorously reviewed by experts to ensure the highest quality product and presentation. Because we are committed to serving our readers' needs, we welcome your feedback on how we can improve future editions of this book.

Cover design by RIPE Creative, Inc.

Printed in the United States of America

ISBN 978-1-61632-953-2

14 13 12   5 4 3

Library of Congress Cataloging-in-Publication Data

Mighell, Tom.
   iPad in one hour for lawyers / Tom Mighell.
     p. cm.
   ISBN 978-1-61632-953-2
  1. iPad (Computer) 2. Practice of law—United States—Data processing. 3. Lawyers—United States—Handbooks, manuals, etc. I. Title.
   KF320.A9M48   2011
   004.16—dc22

                                            2011011978

Discounts are available for books ordered in bulk. Special consideration is given to state bars, CLE programs, and other bar-related organizations. Inquire at Book Publishing, American Bar Association, 321 N. Clark Street, Chicago, Illinois 60654.

Table of Contents

About the Author

Tom Mighell is a Senior Consultant with Contoural, Inc., where he helps companies deal with their records management and electronic discovery capabilities. Tom is a frequent speaker and writer on the Internet, electronic discovery, and other legal technology issues. He has published *The Mighell Marker, a Legal Technology Weekly*, since 2000, and the legal technology blog Inter Alia (**www.inter-alia.net**) since 2002. He is the coauthor, along with Dennis Kennedy, of *The Lawyer's Guide to Collaboration Tools and Technologies: Smart Ways to Work Together*, published by the ABA's Law Practice Management Section. He is also the Co-Host of The Kennedy-Mighell Report, a legal technology podcast produced by The Legal Talk Network.

Tom served on the ABA TECHSHOW planning board for five years, and as the Chair of ABA TECHSHOW 2008. He is currently the Chair-Elect of the ABA's Law Practice Management Section, and will serve as Chair during 2011–2012. Tom received both his B.A. (1987) and his J.D. (1990) degrees from the University of Texas at Austin.

Acknowledgments

To Tim Johnson and the fantastic LPM Publishing staff, for your professionalism and wonderful support; to all my friends in the Law Practice Management Section, for making a technology geek like me feel welcome; and to Kenny, for putting up with my constant obsession for having the latest gadgets—including the iPad, of course.

Introduction—Getting Started

Congratulations on the purchase of your new iPad! You are now the owner of the device that started a revolution in tablet computing; by the time you read this, other competitors will have tablets on the market, offering devices built on the Android, Windows, and even Black-Berry platform. For the purposes of this book, however, we'll be discussing all iPad, all the time.

Your iPad is a powerful device. It allows you to do a lot of things you used to do on your laptop or desktop—surf the web, read your email, type notes or documents—but it can do so much *more*, and all in a contraption that weighs less than a hardcover book. So let's get started!

About This Book

But first, a quick word about the contents of this book. I only have an hour to share some quick iPad lessons, so I really need to make my time with you count. Therefore, I tried to appeal to all types of iPad users: those of you who are tech-proficient, and those of you who might need a little extra help with your new iPad. The first few lessons will be more basic, addressing the setup and overall management of your iPad. The remaining lessons will cover specific ways to be productive with your iPad, including apps specifically designed for practicing lawyers. It may take you slightly *more* than an hour to make it through all six lessons—I hope you don't hold that against me!

In *Beyond the Lessons*, I'll provide you with a lot of the detail I didn't include in the Lessons: finger moves and shortcuts, advanced email settings, and my recommendations of some of the best Apps for your iPad.

Getting Started

Before you start the lessons in this book, it's a good idea to make sure you've completed the following basic steps:

- **Purchase your iPad!** I assume you have already actually bought your iPad by the time you're ready to start the lessons in this book. It doesn't matter whether you purchased the Wi-Fi-only or Wi-Fi/3G version of the iPad, or whether you own the 16, 32 or 64GB models. You may have the original iPad, or are a proud owner of the latest iPad 2. The lessons apply no matter the type of iPad you own.

- **Install iTunes on your computer.** Your iPad uses Apple's iTunes software to sync with your computer, and transfer files, music, and videos to the device. If you haven't already, visit **http://www.apple .com/itunes**, download, and install the iTunes software. For instructions on installing iTunes, check out this article at Dummies.com: **http://www.dummies.com/how-to/content/setting-up-itunes-for-windows.html**.

- **Set up Your iPad in iTunes.** Once iTunes is installed on your computer, connect your iPad to the computer using the cable that came in the box. Every time you connect the iPad to your computer, iTunes will automatically start. To configure the synchronization settings for your iPad, select the iPad under Devices on the left-hand side (your iPad must be connected, or it will not appear in the Devices menu), and you'll be presented with a number of tabs. From here you can manage the media that you put on your device:
  - ▶ **Summary**—basics about your iPad—serial number, whether it has the latest software update, how to reinstall the software, general options, etc.
  - ▶ **Info**—configuring your iPad to sync mail, contacts or calendars. *See Beyond the Lessons for specific instructions on using this page.*

▶ **Apps**—all of the apps currently installed on your iPad, including a listing of those that support File Sharing. You can manage your apps from this page—see *Lesson 3: Multitasking and Folders.*

▶ The remaining tabs allow you to configure synchronization options for:

  • Music

  • Movies

  • TV Shows

  • Podcasts

  • Books

  • Photos

■ **Sync Your iPad with iTunes.** Once you have adjusted these options to your liking, click the **Apply** button, and then press **Sync.** Your iPad will take care of the rest!

■ **Configure Your Security Options.** Security is a serious matter, so before you start using your iPad you want to make sure it's secure in the event it's lost or stolen. See *Beyond the Lessons* for instructions for configuring the security settings on your new device.

■ **Charge the iPad Battery.** To charge the battery, connect the iPad to a power outlet using the included cable and the 10W USB power adapter. You can also connect to a high-power USB port with the included cable, but it might take longer to charge. If you do not connect to a *high-power* port, you may see a "Not Charging" message; some USB ports and accessories do not provide enough power to charge an iPad. The fastest way to charge is using the 10W adapter—even so, it will take several hours to charge the internal battery.

■ **Connect to the Internet.** If you have an iPad with 3G, you should be connected automatically. To connect via Wi-Fi, follow these instructions:

- ▶ First, make sure you're in an area with a wireless connection.
- ▶ Press *Settings*, then *Wi-Fi*, and make sure *Wi-Fi* is in the ON position.
- ▶ A list of available networks will appear below. Select the network to which you want to connect. If the network requires a password, you'll be prompted to enter it.
- ▶ You're connected!
- **Start Buying Apps.** If you're not familiar with the iPhone or iPad, you'll quickly learn that these devices do not have "programs" as you might think of them on your computer. Instead, the iPad uses *apps*, short for applications. These are self-contained programs specifically designed for the iPad. Your iPad comes with several default applications, but if you really want to get anything done on your new device you'll want to immediately start downloading your favorite apps from the iPad App Store. Learn more about how to do this, as well as browse a list of great iPad apps for lawyers, in *Beyond the Lessons*.

Once you've completed these steps, you are ready to move on to the lessons in this book. Some of the lessons are relatively short, while others are longer. But we've got a lot to cover in just one hour. So if you're ready, let's get started!

Navigating Your iPad and Browsing the Web

I always like to start exploring a new device by understanding its features, so let's take a quick walking tour of your new iPad (see Figure 1):

Figure 1

A. **On/Off button**—to turn the iPad on, just press and hold the On/Off button. To turn it off, press the On/Off button until the **slide to power off** screen appears. The On/Off button will also put the iPad to sleep if you press it once.

B. **Screen Rotation Lock/Mute**—in older versions of the iPad, this button would lock the screen so it would not rotate when you turned from landscape to portrait mode. When the iOS4.2 upgrade was installed, it turned the button into a Mute feature, to mute all sound coming from the device. Due to complaints, the iPad 2 allows users the option of making this button *either* the Screen Rotation Lock or Mute function.

C/D. **Volume**—press the top half of this switch to turn up the volume, and the bottom half to lower it. If you press the lower half for a second or two, you automatically mute it. You'll see a volume graphic onscreen to let you know where you are in terms of loudness.

E. **Headphone Jack**—this is where you plug your earbuds or headphones to watch videos or listen to tunes on the iPad's iPod or in music apps like **Pandora**.

F. **Dock Connector**—here's where you plug the USB cable in to connect your iPad to your computer for syncing, or to a power outlet for charging. The Dock Connector is where you would connect an external keyboard as well.

G. **Microphone**—used for dictating voice memos, or other apps that need to "listen" to what's going on.

H. Speakers—where you hear any sound projected from the iPad.

I. **Home Button**—the only button on the iPad, it has a few functions. First, it *always* takes you Home—the first screen. You can also use the Home button to:

■ Move to another program—just press the button, go back to the main iPad screen, and tap open another program.

- Go home, fast—If you're on a faraway screen, double-click the Home button and you'll immediately be taken there.
- Search your iPad—after you get to the Home screen, click the Home button again and you'll wind up at the **Search** page, where you can search through stuff on your iPad.

The iPad's Default Apps

When you first turn on your iPad, you'll notice that it comes with several apps or features already installed. They include:

- **Calendar**—learn how to set up this calendar in *Lesson 2*.
- **Contacts**—easy access to all your contacts—learn how to set them up in *Lesson 2*.
- **Notes**—a basic, simple note-taking app (read about better note apps in *Lesson 5*).
- **Maps**—search for addresses and get directions here.
- **Videos**—press this button to access any videos that may be stored on your iPad.
- **YouTube**—watch and explore YouTube videos here.
- **iTunes**—explore the iTunes store and download music, books, or videos directly to your iPad.
- **App Store**—browse for the latest apps and download them to your iPad, all with the click of a button.
- **Settings**—where all the magic happens; the place to configure your iPad and all of its apps.
- **Safari**—the iPad's built-in web browser.
- **Email**—access your messages here (and learn how to set up your email in *Lesson 2*).
- **Photos**—press this button to view all the photos stored on your device.
- **iPod**—similar to the iPhone or iPod, this is where you can access music, audiobooks, podcasts, and other audio files.

Browsing the Web

To get onto the Web, just press the *Safari* button (icon) on your Home screen. The first time you do this, you'll see a blank window, ready for your instructions. Tap the address bar above, and the iPad keyboard will pop up. Enter in the URL of the site you want to visit. Alternatively, tap your finger in the Search box in the upper-right, and enter some search terms; by default, Google is your search engine (you can change the default search engine in Safari Settings).

Safari acts mostly like the browser on your computer, but with fewer buttons (see Figure 2).

Figure 2

- The sideways triangles send you Back and Forward, to move back and forth between web pages.
- The next icon is called the "Page Juggler." Safari can keep up to nine web pages open at a time, and you access them here.
- The next button helps you access your Bookmarks, bringing up a list of your saved bookmarks.
- The ➦ sign allows you to add a bookmark, either to your Home Screen or list of saved bookmarks.
- Within the Address Bar, you'll see either an X or a circular arrow. Click on the X to interrupt the download of a web page, or click the arrow to refresh the page you're already viewing.

When you first open a web page, you can see the whole page, not just part of it. To see the page up close, you need to use your fingers to zoom in. There are three ways to do this: 1) rotate your screen from Portrait to Landscape mode; 2) do the "two-finger spread;" or 3) simply tap twice. Learn more about these shortcuts in *Beyond the Lessons.*

Once you have browsed a few web pages, you may be ready to save some of them as bookmarks. When you tap the Add Bookmark button, you'll have a few options: to add the bookmark, add the page to your Home Screen, or mail a link to that particular page. For now, let's just select **Add Bookmark.** When you do, the following will appear (see Figure 3):

Figure 3

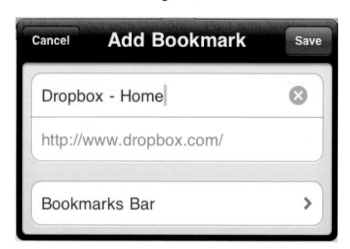

You can customize the name of your bookmark here, and then specify where you want the bookmark to go—on the Bookmarks Bar (which appears right below the Address Bar in your browser, for easy access), or within a particular folder. Then click Save, and you're done.

To manage your bookmarks, tap on the Bookmarks button and then tap **Edit.** You can do a few things here:

■ Tap on **New Folder** to create a topical folder to better manage your bookmarks.

- Tap on the Red Circle to delete the bookmark.
- Tap on the bookmark itself to edit the name or URL of the bookmark.
- Tap and hold on the lines to move the bookmark up or down to another location.

That's it! Now you can start surfing the Web, and bookmark any sites you want to visit later.

Setting Up Mail, Calendar, and Contacts

The life blood of a lawyer's practice arguably can be found in three types of digital data—email, calendar, and contacts. Being able to access all of these important things on your iPad no doubt will be one of your first priorities upon turning on the device, so in this lesson I'll show you how to do just that.

Your Mail, Calendar, and Contacts are configured through the *Settings* app, which is on the Home screen. Just press *Settings* and you'll see a wide range of options (see Figure 4).

Figure 4

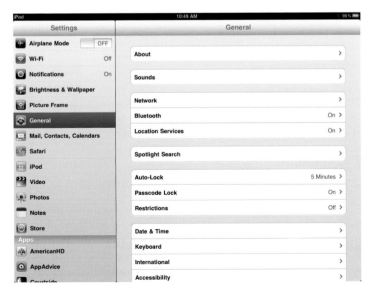

Here, you can configure most of the features of your iPad—Wi-Fi, how you receive notifications, your wallpaper, and individual settings for many of the apps on your device. For purposes of this lesson, we'll focus on the *Mail, Contacts, Calendars* settings, so click that now (see Figure 5).

Figure 5

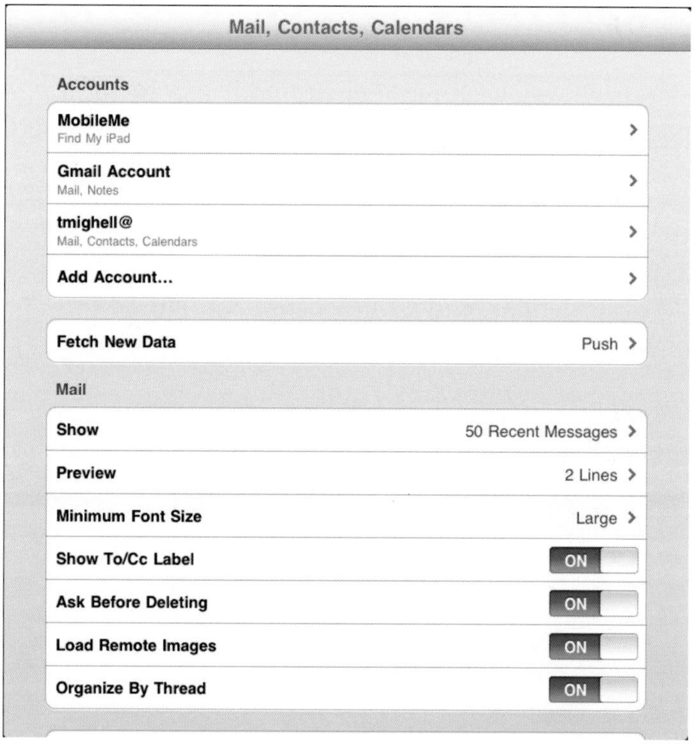

Mail, Contacts, Calendars

Accounts

MobileMe
Find My iPad   >

Gmail Account
Mail, Notes   >

tmighell@
Mail, Contacts, Calendars   >

Add Account...   >

Fetch New Data   Push >

Mail

Show   50 Recent Messages >

Preview   2 Lines >

Minimum Font Size   Large >

Show To/Cc Label   ON

Ask Before Deleting   ON

Load Remote Images   ON

Organize By Thread   ON

Tap *Add Account* . . .
On the next screen, you're given a menu of different types of accounts to add. They are:
- Microsoft Exchange
- MobileMe
- Gmail

- Yahoo!
- AOL
- Other

The following are quick instructions on setting up the most popular email services.

Microsoft Exchange

If you use Exchange to manage your mail, contacts and calendars, it's very simple to connect your iPad to an existing account:

- *Click on Microsoft Exchange*
- *Enter your email address*
- *Enter your Domain* (this is optional; if you don't have one, don't worry)
- *Enter the Username and Password on your account*
- *Enter a Description for the account*, if you want
- *Press Next*
- *If you get a message "Cannot Verify Server Identity," press Continue*
- *If you get a message "Unable to Verify Certificate," press Accept*
- *A field labeled Server will appear below email—enter your Exchange server information*
- *Press Next*
- *If you get a message "Unable to Verify Certificate" again, don't worry—just go ahead and press Accept*

You'll now be asked what information you want to synchronize between your iPad and Exchange: *Mail, Contacts, and Calendar*. If you select Calendar and Contacts, you'll get a message asking you whether you want to *keep* or *delete* the local data on your device. Because this is likely the first time you have synced your iPad, there probably isn't

13

any local data. So select either *Keep* to preserve your existing contacts or calendar items, or *Delete* to get rid of any contacts or calendar items that currently exist on your device.

Press *Save*, and your device is now configured to accept Mail, Contacts and Calendar items from your Exchange server.

MobileMe

Apple's MobileMe product allows you to sync your mail, contacts and calendar across all of your devices, whether you have a Mac, PC, iPhone or iPad. If you already have a MobileMe account, just enter your Apple login information. If you don't have an Apple login (but you should already, especially if you set up iTunes), just press the button *Create Free Apple ID*.

The screen that follows your login is fairly basic, asking whether you want to sync *Mail, Contacts, Calendars* or *Bookmarks*. Select the items you want to sync, and press *Save*. Your data will be available on your iPad as soon as the device finishes its initial over-the-air sync with MobileMe.

Gmail and Yahoo!

If you have one or more Gmail or Yahoo! accounts, the configuration options are identical. Here's how to access these webmail services on the iPad:

- Enter your Name
- Enter your Gmail or Yahoo! email address
- Enter your Password
- Enter a Description, if you want
- Press Next
- On the next screen, select whether you want to sync your Mail, Calendars, or Notes
- Press Save

AOL

If you're still using AOL mail, tap on the AOL button and follow these instructions:

- Enter your Name
- Enter your AOL email address
- Enter your Password
- Enter a Description, if you want
- Press Next
- Select whether to sync Mail, Notes, or both
- Press Save

If you don't use any of these email services, all is not lost—just press *Other* and follow the directions for setting up any other type of email (See *Beyond the Lessons* for instructions on setting up other email types, as well as setting up your email, calendars and contacts from within iTunes).

The Rest of the Options

Now that you've set up your email account(s), you still have some other decisions to make. In the Mail, Contacts and Calendars area there are a good number of settings to configure. Explanations for these settings can be found in *Beyond the Lessons*; be sure to read up on these settings once you have more time to play with your iPad.

Using the Universal Inbox

One of the great additions to the iPad (depending on how you like to use email, that is) is the Universal Inbox. When you go to the Mail app in Landscape view, you'll see a list of all your email accounts in the left pane. At the top is an option for *All Inboxes*, which will take you to your Universal Inbox—a view that displays all email from each of the accounts you configured on your iPad, received in chronological order from newest to oldest.

If you want to view email from a specific account, you'll find inboxes for each of them listed under your Universal Inbox. Just press on the Inbox you want to use. To dig more deeply into a particular email account and any folders you may have created, make a selection under the *Accounts* section. There you'll see a full listing of all the folders you've created for that account.

Managing Your iPad: Multitasking and Folders

Now that you've got your iPad up and running and your mail and calendar are all set up, it's time to start getting organized. In this lesson, we'll talk about multitasking with your iPad, as well as how to organize your apps within folders.

Multitasking. One of the great limitations of the iPad when it was first released was the inability to organize content on it, or work on different applications without first closing one and opening another. This "anti-multitasking" approach initially taken by Apple had a simple enough explanation: working within a single app allows a person to be more focused, efficient, and productive. Besides, multitasking is for geeks, right?

Users soon found some serious drawbacks to the lack of multitasking on the iPad. It was impossible to listen to music from apps like Pandora and work in other apps at the same time. If you were having an instant messaging conversation with someone and had to go check your email, when you came back the IM program had to start up all over again.

Apple finally saw the light, and today's iPad operating system allows multitasking, although it's probably not exactly what you're used to on your personal computer. Moving between programs on your iPad is pretty simple—here's how:

- When you're working in one app and need to move to another, simply press the Home Button twice.
- The open application will move up, exposing a list of all running applications along the bottom of the screen.
- If you want to go back to the app you were using, just press the Home button twice again, and the multitasking bar will disappear.
- To open another running application, just tap on that application's icon on the multitasking bar.
- If you can't see the running app on the screen, just swipe the bar to the left, and you'll see other apps that may be open. The multitasking bar displays seven currently-running apps in Landscape mode, six apps in Portrait mode.

When you're not using these open apps, they exist in "suspended" mode; the iPad will keep as many apps running as memory will allow. When you reopen one, it will pick up where you left off the last time you used it.

If the device runs out of memory, however, the iPad will automatically purge apps from their suspended state to free up memory. Unfortunately, you don't have any control over that process, but you can definitely control the number of apps that are open at any one time.

To "quit" apps that are running, press and hold on any app icon in the multitasking bar until the icons begin to jiggle. A red minus sign will appear in the upper left-hand corner of each icon—just press there to remove the app from the list and terminate it.

Folders. As you begin to accumulate apps, you'll find the number of screens increasing. The iPad simply adds a newly-installed app to the end of the list, and keeps on going, without any rhyme or reason. Unfortunately, there *is* a limit; currently iPad users are limited to 11 screens. With 20 apps per screen, plus the 5 apps that appear at the bottom, the maximum number of apps is 225.

Some of you will never come close to having 200 apps on your iPad, but I'll bet that many of you will—after all, with all the great free apps out there, it's easy to get carried away. Even if you don't have that many apps, having too many screens to page through and search for your apps can be a real hassle. You can always use the Search function to look for a particular app (to access Search, press the Home button once to get to the Home screen, then press it once more, or swipe to the right), but wouldn't it be great if there was a better way to organize all of those apps?

Fortunately, there is, and it's ridiculously simple. The iPad allows you to create folders on your device that hold up to 20 apps. Here's how to do it:

- Press down and hold an app you want to move into a folder until it (and the other apps) start to jiggle.
- Move the app's icon on top of another app that you want to include in the same folder.
- A folder will instantly be created, containing those two apps.
- Your iPad will automatically name the folder based on the content of the apps. If you like the name, just press the Home button and your folder is complete. If you want to change the name, just type in the space listing the current name and edit the title. Then press the Home button to finish.
- Adding other apps is easy—while the apps are in "jiggle" mode, just tap and hold on one of them, and drag it over the folder you've created.
- If the app you're moving into a folder is on a different screen from the folder itself, you can drag the icon left or right, depending on where the folder is located, and go from screen to screen until you reach the screen with the desired folder.

You can set up folders for News, Entertainment, Games, Travel, Productivity, and any other category you like. To access the apps in a folder, press on that folder—it will unfold and display all of the apps contained within it.

Managing Apps in iTunes

Moving around all of your apps on the iPad can be time-consuming, and not very efficient. Fortunately, there's a way to manage and organize your apps in iTunes that's much easier, especially if you're more comfortable using a mouse to move things around. Here's how to do it.

   Make sure your iPad is connected to your computer, and then in iTunes click on your iPad under the *Devices* entry on the left. When you get to the iPad's main screen in iTunes, one of the options at the top is *Apps*; click it. You'll be presented with two views: a listing of all of your apps on the left, and then screenshots of your iPad screens on the right (see Figure 6).

Figure 6

To move apps from screen to screen, just select the app you want to move and drag it down to the screen of your choice. The view at the top will change to that screen, and you will then be able to place the app icon anywhere on that screen. To move it into a folder, simply hold the app over the desired folder; the folder will open up, and you can place the app icon anywhere within the folder you choose.

If you no longer want to keep an app on your iPad, there are a couple ways to get rid of it:

- On your iPad, press and hold the app's icon until it begins to jiggle; there will be a black "X" mark in the upper-left corner. Press the X mark, and you'll be asked to confirm the deletion.
- Within iTunes, scroll down the list of apps on the left side of the Apps page, and uncheck the app you want removed from the iPad.
- Note: neither of these options deletes the app from your computer—to do that, you'll need to click on the *Apps* link under the *Library* area on your iTunes left-hand menu. From there, you can right-click on any app, select Delete, and you'll have the option of removing it completely from your computer.

Adding Files to Your iPad and Syncing Them

As much as I love the iPad, even I must admit that one of its biggest drawbacks is that it cannot store files in a way that we might recognize from our PCs, or even on our Macs. There are no document folders on the iPad, so there is no way for you yourself to store or organize your documents, spreadsheets, presentations, images, videos, or other types of files. Instead, you must access those files through the individual apps on the device. Further, there's no good way to physically transfer the files; the iPad has no USB port to which a computer or hard drive could be connected nor an SD card slot for additional storage.

But do not lose heart—there are ways to transfer files between your iPad and your computer that do not rely on USB ports or SD cards, and in this lesson we will discuss two of those ways: 1) file sharing in iTunes, and 2) using cloud-based apps to access your files.

Sharing Files Between Your iPad and a Computer

Transferring files between your iPad and your computer is actually very easy, although it's not terribly intuitive. Because the iPad syncs with iTunes, you must use iTunes to transfer files between the device and your computer. Another caveat is that you will only be able to transfer files from apps that support "File Sharing." Fortunately, more and more apps are supporting File Sharing, especially those apps that deal with documents and files. However, files can only be opened by apps that support the particular file type; so before transferring files as described below, make sure you understand the file types that are supported by all of your iPad apps.

Here's how to copy files using File Sharing:

- Connect the iPad to your computer.
- Launch iTunes (you must be using iTunes 9.1 or later to take advantage of File Sharing).
- Once iTunes connects with your iPad, select it from the Devices section, on the left.
- Click the **Apps** button across the top, to see all of the apps currently installed on your device.
- Scroll down below the apps, to the section marked *File Sharing* (see Figure 7). There you will find a listing of all of your applications that support File Sharing. If you do not see the File Sharing section, that means you don't currently have any apps that support File Sharing.

Figure 7

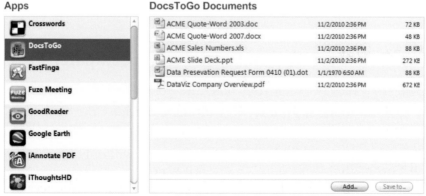

File Sharing

The apps listed below can transfer documents between your iPad and this computer.

Apps	DocsToGo Documents		
Crosswords	ACME Quote-Word 2003.doc	11/2/2010 2:36 PM	72 KB
DocsToGo	ACME Quote-Word 2007.docx	11/2/2010 2:36 PM	48 KB
FastFinga	ACME Sales Numbers.xls	11/2/2010 2:36 PM	88 KB
Fuze Meeting	ACME Slide Deck.ppt	11/2/2010 2:36 PM	272 KE
GoodReader	Data Presevation Request Form 0410 (01).dot	1/1/1970 6:50 AM	88 KB
Google Earth	DataViz Company Overview.pdf	11/2/2010 2:36 PM	672 KE
iAnnotate PDF			
iThoughtsHD			

Add... Save to...

- Click on an application. You will see a listing of all the documents being stored by that application to the right.

At this point, you have a couple of options, depending on whether you want to transfer a document *to* or *from* the iPad:

- To add a document <u>to</u> your iPad:
  - ▶ Make sure you have selected the correct app under File Sharing.
  - ▶ Click the Add button; a dialog box will appear, allowing you to navigate to the document you want to add. Again, make sure you select only files supported by that particular app.
  - ▶ If you already have the folder open, you can simply drag and drop the file(s) onto the Documents list to copy them automatically to the app.
- To move documents <u>from</u> your iPad to the computer:
  - ▶ Make sure you have selected the correct app under File Sharing.
  - ▶ Highlight the file you want to move, and then click the *Save to . . .* button. Locate the folder on your computer that you want to move the file to, and click *Choose* to save the file.
  - ▶ If the destination folder on your computer is already open, you can just drag and drop the file(s) into that folder.

Another Way to Access Files: Through the Cloud

If using iTunes to transfer files is a hassle for you, there's an even easier way to transfer and access files on your iPad. By taking advantage of apps that store your files in the "cloud," you can wirelessly transfer documents and other files directly to your iPad.

Rather than go into a long discussion to define "cloud computing," I'll simplify it by saying that the term refers to apps and services that store your data on other computers (otherwise known as "the cloud"). They provide access to this data from anywhere you can find online access. If you use webmail like Gmail or Yahoo!, you're using a cloud computing service. The fact that the iPad cannot connect to your computer via USB (or anything other than iTunes) means it is particularly suited to working with cloud computing services.

There are dozens of iPad apps that allow you to access files on the Internet. I'll only focus on a few that I have used and would recommend.

The first is **Dropbox (http://db.tt/JCp3V5J)**, an easy-to-use service that allows you to sync your files online, and across all of your computers. To get started with Dropbox, you'll first need to download the application to your computer; there are versions for Windows, Mac and Linux platforms. Once it's installed, Dropbox simply creates a new folder on your computer—"My Dropbox." Just drag files and folders into the My Dropbox folder, and they are automatically synced to your online account. Your files are also automatically updated whenever you make changes to them.

Once you've installed Dropbox on one computer, install it on another computer that you use. Now you can access all of your Dropbox files, no matter which computer you happen to be using. Dropbox can also share files with other people, so you can work on documents together or provide access to files for others to view. A free Dropbox account provides 2GB of online storage, with up to 100GB available for a reasonable monthly fee.

Now that you've got Dropbox installed, it's time to install it on your iPad (Dropbox is also available on the iPhone, BlackBerry, and Android). Go to the iPad App Store and search for Dropbox—the download is free. Once you've entered your login information, you'll have access to your entire My Dropbox folder—and all of your files and documents—right there on your iPad (see Figure 8).

Figure 8

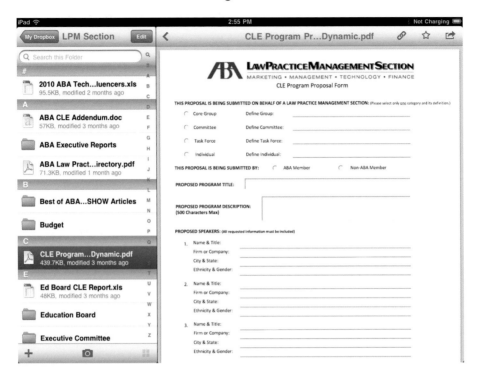

Just select any document to view it—Dropbox will let you view just about any type of document, whether it's a spreadsheet, PDF file, presentation, or image. If you want to edit any of the documents in your Dropbox, there's bad news and good news. The bad news is editing is not available in Dropbox. The good news is that there are a number of apps that work directly with Dropbox to help you edit your documents. One such app is called **Documents To Go**; you can open a Dropbox document up in the DocsToGo app, make your edits, and have those edits saved back to your Dropbox folders. I'll talk more about DocsToGo in the next chapter.

In those iPad apps that connect with other apps, like Dropbox and DocsToGo above, you'll find this icon ⬆ somewhere on the screen.

Press it, and you'll get a listing of all the apps that will open the file you have selected.

Two other reputable services offering the same features as Dropbox are **SugarSync (www.sugarsync.com)** and **Box.net (www.box.net)**. Both services also have comparable iPad apps, so you can access all of your desktop or laptop files on your iPad using these tools as well. There are also other apps in the App Store offering file management services; spend some time browsing the selections there before making a final decision on which service is best for you.

Another well-regarded app that helps you manage your files is called **Air Sharing**. This app incorporates remote file access, wireless file sharing, an advanced PDF viewer and wireless printing. You'll need to do some set up before you can access your files remotely, such as enter your Dropbox or MobileMe information, so the app can connect to those services.

Other File Management Tips

Backing Up Your Files. iTunes automatically performs a backup of your iPad, including your shared files, each time it syncs with your computer. The files you access using Dropbox, SugarSync and the like are backed up by those services as well as by iTunes. Unfortunately, if you lose a file, you cannot selectively restore it from a backup; you will have to completely restore your iPad to get that document back. So it's a good idea to frequently back up the files you have created on your iPad to a folder on your computer.

Deleting Apps. If you delete an app from your iPad, you'll also be deleting all the files on the iPad associated with the app. That's why backing up your shared files is so important, especially before you delete the app from the iPad—see above.

Removing Files from Your iPad. If you have a file you no longer need, there are two ways to delete it from your iPad:

- First, determine whether the app itself allows you to delete files. In most apps you can find this out simply by swiping the particular file to the right—a red DELETE button will appear if the app supports deletion. Just press that button to delete the file.

- If the app in question does not support deletion, you'll need to remove the file from within iTunes.
  - ▶ Connect the iPad to your computer and start iTunes
  - ▶ Select the iPad in the Devices section on the left, and click on the Apps tab.
  - ▶ Scroll down to the File Sharing section, and select the application from which you want to delete the file.
  - ▶ From the list of files that appears in the Documents list to the right, highlight the file you want to delete.
  - ▶ Press the **Delete** key on your keyboard. You'll be prompted onscreen to confirm the deletion.
  - ▶ The file will be immediately deleted from your iPad.

Being Productive on the iPad

With the first four lessons, you should now have your iPad set up and ready to use. You've configured your email, calendar and contacts, learned how to multitask and organize your apps into folders, and mastered the art of transferring files between your iPad and computer. Now it's time to get to work, and learn how to really *use* the iPad in your work or law practice.

Some claim the iPad was really initially designed for content *consumption*, not content *creation*. Indeed, there are hundreds of fantastic apps that allow you to read books, magazines, and news; connect with your friends on social networking sites; educate school kids about different subjects; and play games. These apps just feel *right* on the iPad.

There are also a large number of content creation apps available—we've seen an explosion in the number of artists and photographers using the iPad to create amazing works of art, through content creation apps designed specifically for the device, just to name one example. But using a tablet computer for a lawyer's prime activity—drafting documents—may feel a bit awkward for some. Lawyers may not feel comfortable using the on-screen keyboard to tap out notes or even write a letter to a client. This is one reason why some lawyers initially viewed the iPad with skepticism as a tool for practicing law.

In this Lesson, I'll try to dispel that reluctance to see the iPad as a content creation tool, and look directly at some of the ways lawyers can use the device to write notes, documents, spreadsheets, and even presentations. I'll also share some of my favorite ways that lawyers can conduct meetings, brainstorm, and review legal research, all on the iPad.

Before You Start. One of the reasons we don't think of the iPad as a content creation device is that as a tablet, it's tough to actually *get content into* the thing. True enough—but that doesn't mean we're completely limited to using the iPad alone. Let's look at a few tools that can help you level the playing field when it comes to content creation. Because we only have an hour together in this book, I'll mention just a few of my favorites, and leave it to you to explore the other options.

Keyboard. A keyboard, you ask? Surely not. The whole *point* of a tablet computer is to do away with the keyboard. And you'd be right. But if you're truly interested in using the iPad for content creation, and even potentially as a laptop replacement, you *must* have a physical keyboard. Fortunately, there are number of terrific options available (see Figure 9).

Figure 9

The first is from Apple itself. The **Apple Wireless Keyboard**
(**http://bit.ly/9jTTxM**) connects to your iPad using a Bluetooth connection; here's how to "pair" the keyboard with your device:

- Make sure the keyboard is turned on (the wireless keyboard is
  battery-powered).
- On the iPad, go to *Settings*, then *General*, then *Bluetooth*.
- Make sure that the Bluetooth option is turned *ON*. When it is,
  it will begin searching for Bluetooth-enabled devices, and list
  them under Devices. Your Keyboard should be listed there
  (see Figure 10).

Figure 10

- You will be prompted by the iPad with a message to type a series
  of numbers on the keyboard. Type those numbers and press *Enter*
  on the keyboard.
- Your wireless keyboard is now "paired" with the iPad, and you
  can begin to use it immediately.

Among other wireless keyboards, I'm intrigued by the ZAGGmate
cover with keyboard (**http://www.zagg.com/accessories/zaggmate.php**).

It's an aluminum cover that connects to your iPad to seal it up tight. When you open the cover, it unfolds to provide a keyboard and back-rest for the iPad.

Stand. If you don't buy a keyboard with a dock, or even if you just want something to prop up your iPad when you're reading or looking at a photo slideshow, you're going to need some sort of stand. Plus, although the iPad is a lot lighter than your average laptop, it's still going to feel pretty heavy in your hands if you hold it for an hour or two. That's why having a stand as a backup is a good idea. There are dozens of stands available; you can find some of them at the Apple Store (**http://store.apple.com**), or at the iLounge (**http://www.ilounge.com**), a review site for iPad and other accessories. There are also a number of cases that serve as stands—you'll want to review them too.

My stand of choice is the **Twelve South Compass (http://twelve south.com/products/compass/)** portable stand. It looks a bit like an easel, allowing you to display the iPad in either Portrait or Landscape mode, and type away with your wireless keyboard. There's also a fold-away secondary leg that can be used to create a workstation, angled just right for typing on the onscreen keyboard (if you want to do that). The best part about the Compass is its size; when folded up it's 7 inches long by 1 inch wide, making it easy to store and transport anywhere. A word of caution, however—on x-ray the Compass can look a little like a sharp object, so when you're traveling through airport security, you will probably want to take it out of your bag and put it one of the security bins.

Stylus. Many people (myself included) purchased the iPad with the intent of using it as a true "tablet" device—that is, to use it like I would a paper tablet, and take notes at meetings, interviews, and the like. Unfortunately, a stylus wasn't a good fit for me; my handwriting is simply not good enough, and I type much faster than I write. But if you are comfortable with writing, you *must* take advantage of the iPad's ability to capture written notes. And finding the right stylus is the first place to start.

Like stands and cases, there are a number of different styluses available for the iPad. One thing they all have in common is the tip. An iPad touch screen won't respond to a hard, pointy stylus. Go ahead, try it—try to write on the screen with the hard end of a ball point pen, and it won't work. That's because the iPad's screen is known as a "capacitive touch screen," which means that the display relies on the electrical properties of the human body to detect when and where on a display the user is touching. In order to write effectively on the iPad's screen, the tip of the stylus must mimic the consistency of your fingertip. So the stylus you buy will either come with a foam-like or rubber tip. Again, there are number of stylus types available for you out there; do your research and find the one that works best for you. I have tried both the **Pogo Sketch (http://tenonedesign.com/sketch.php)** and the **Boxwave Capacitive Stylus (http://bit.ly/azFZif)** and I like them both.

Of course, you can take notes with your finger, as well. Some of the apps mentioned below allow fingertip note-taking, although you might want to use a stylus if you need more control over what you're writing.

Printer. Once you've taken your notes, you might want to print them out. To do this, you'll need to use AirPrint, an iPad feature that allows you to print wirelessly to a compatible printer. You can access the Print option in those apps that support printing; to see if an app supports printing, press the Share button and look for the Print or Print File option.

To print from your iPad, you'll also need a printer that supports the AirPrint feature. As of this writing, there are 18 AirPrint-enabled printers, all from HP. To see the latest printers with AirPrint functionality, read the Apple KnowledgeBase article at **http://support.apple.com/ kb/ht4356**. Once you have such a printer, press the Print or Print File button in your iPad app, and you'll see a box like Figure 11:

Figure 11

Press Select Printer to choose the printer, then tap to select the page range and number of copies. After you press Print, your printer should begin to print out the file from your iPad.

Getting Started: Taking Notes

Before we graduate to full document preparation, let's start with the basics, and take some notes. There are many different note taking iPad apps, all with varying levels of features. Here are a few apps I've tried out, with their features, pros, and cons.

Note Taker HD

- Features
  - ▸ Designed for finger or stylus use
  - ▸ Easy to create notes in various styles
  - ▸ Save to PDF
- Pros
  - ▸ Pretty intuitive note-taker
  - ▸ Small feature set makes it easy to understand and use
- Cons
  - ▸ Will not save PDF files to Dropbox, Evernote, or other services
  - ▸ Small feature set means limited capabilities
  - ▸ Wrist protection feature makes it difficult to write in the primary editing view

Penultimate

- Features
  - ▸ Multiple Notebooks
  - ▸ Three types of paper on each page—graph, lined, or plain
  - ▸ Eraser to get rid of notes you don't want
  - ▸ Take notes in different colors and pen thicknesses
  - ▸ Ability to send notebooks as PDF, or download to iTunes
- Pros
  - ▸ Easy to understand note-taking app
  - ▸ Wrist protection allows you to rest your wrist on the corner while you're writing
  - ▸ Eraser will eliminate those messy pages or mistakes
- Cons
  - ▸ Limited feature set
  - ▸ Unable to send to other apps like Evernote or GoodReader
  - ▸ Unable to type notes into a notebook
  - ▸ Can only take notes in Portrait mode

WritePad

- Features
  - ▶ Handwriting recognition—will turn your handwriting into type, before your very eyes
  - ▶ Three modes of writing—note pad, split-screen with note pad/type, and keyboard
  - ▶ Export your document to PDF, or share via Email, Twitter, Facebook or Wi-Fi
  - ▶ Syncs with Dropbox, so your documents are automatically uploaded to your Dropbox folder
- Pros
  - ▶ Good for those who don't want to keep handwritten notes, but who would prefer to write than type
- Cons
  - ▶ At times handwriting recognition is great—but sometimes, given time to think, it changes its mind and converts your writing to something different
  - ▶ Going back to correct the mistakes can take longer than typing it out in the first place
  - ▶ Good for short notes or emails, but not long documents

Elements

- Features
  - ▶ Very basic text editor
  - ▶ Syncs all your notes as Text files to your Dropbox account
  - ▶ Multiple type fonts, sizes, and colors
- Pros
  - ▶ Does one thing and does it very well—edit text
  - ▶ Dropbox integration is key to managing notes

- Cons
  - ▶ You cannot write on this app—you must type in your notes
  - ▶ No ability to export your notes in any format other than text

FastFinga

- Features
  - ▶ All finger, all the time—use your finger to take notes—you can use your stylus too, if you want
  - ▶ Multiple options and themes for writing
  - ▶ Export to Twitter, Evernote, Email, PDF, or your Photo Library
- Pros
  - ▶ Tons of features right on the screen
  - ▶ Notes are searchable by Tag or Theme
  - ▶ You can create folders to organize your notes
- Cons
  - ▶ While there are a lot of features, they can be a little overwhelming on the screen—Opt for the Simple Toolbar
  - ▶ The notes screen is not completely intuitive—you write on the bottom half of the screen and see your notes appear on the top. They appear smaller than they actually are.

Document Creation on the iPad

Notes are great to take while in a meeting, interview, deposition, or listening to trial or hearing testimony. But if you have to churn out some serious legal documents, you need a serious word processor. And while the iPad features a number of great word processing applications, none of them are what could truly be called "serious." After all, they're apps, not full-fledged programs. As a result, the feature set and functionality is pretty limited when you compare it to Word, WordPerfect, or Pages for Mac.

Even so, you may find the need to create or simply edit a document, spreadsheet, or presentation on your iPad, and you might not need all the bells and whistles of the major office suites. Here's a complete list (as of this writing) of the iPad's document creation options, and some things to think about before you try them out. Most of these suites are able to create and edit documents, spreadsheets, and presentations, with varying degrees of success.

iWork

Because the iPad is an Apple product, we should start with Apple's productivity suite—it's likely to be the most integrated into the iPad's functionality. **Pages** is Apple's word processing app, and although it offers only a basic subset of features and functions compared to its full-powered Mac brethren, it certainly offers enough to create and edit documents. Templates are available here, but you may be better off starting with a blank document.

Numbers is the app you'll use for creating spreadsheets, and the iPad version packs a surprising amount of power into such a small app. Whether you are a novice or power spreadsheet creator, Numbers has something for everyone. Again, you won't find every feature here that you would on the Mac version, but you can always transfer your document to your computer to modify and improve on it.

It seems that **Keynote** is an app for which the iPad was specifically built—not only can you design and create beautiful presentations on it, you can also use the iPad to present the file you just created. Although you might not find the fantastic graphics effects and customizable transitions of the Mac version, the iPad's Keynote features some terrific multi-step transitions that can be applied with just a few taps. If you rely on speaker's notes during your presentation, however, you may have a problem here; there's no place on the iPad app to create them. Oh well; you needed an excuse to be more extemporaneous in your speaking, right?

For some, iWork's most glaring drawback (if you consider it a drawback) is its conversion of Microsoft Office documents. For now, anyway, most lawyers still use Word, Excel and PowerPoint for their productivity needs. The iWork apps cannot save in Office format, but they can export to their Office file type counterpart. Also unfortunately, while they can import Office 2007 and above documents (those ending in 'x,' such as .docx, .xlsx, and .pptx), they cannot export in those formats. So there may be some reformatting you'll need to do on Office 2007 or 2010 documents you edit in iWork.

Documents to Go

Docs to Go has been around a long time, syncing documents between PDAs, smartphones, and other devices for over a decade. The iPad version comes in two flavors: a basic edition that offers viewing and editing of Word and Excel documents, and a Pro release that adds PowerPoint viewing and editing.

As far as editing goes, you just get the basics with Docs to Go. You can change the Font (only six are available), text, or highlight color, indent and justify text, and create bulleted, numbered, or outline text. The point here is document editing, not formatting—you'll want to use your regular desktop application to "pretty up" the document. Like many document management applications, Docs to Go features an "Open in . . ." option that allows you to open your document in any application on your iPad that supports that file type. A word of caution: if you move a document from Docs to Go to another app, then make edits to that document, you may not be able to transfer that edited document *back* to Docs to Go. Make sure this is possible before attempting significant edits on any documents you transfer out of the program.

A must-have feature of these document and file apps is the ability to access your files in "the cloud," and Docs to Go does not disappoint. You can sync your files located in Google Docs, Box.net, Dropbox, Apple's iDisk and SugarSync. All you do is configure the services you have with Documents to Go, and they will automatically appear on your iPad when you are ready to view or edit them. You can also download the free desktop sync tool, which allows you to pick a folder on your computer and sync the documents inside to your iPad, or sync with iTunes if you prefer.

As with most of these applications, Docs to Go isn't perfect; there are a few shortcomings. For example, you can view attachments to email you receive on the iPad, but you cannot edit them. Also, the Search feature will only search for document names—you cannot search within documents, unless you're in the specific document itself. Finally, Docs to Go seems suited more for individual users, with a lack of support for enterprise use. If you want to use this app as part of a networked computer environment at your firm or company, you will want to check with the IT department to make sure it will work with your current document management systems.

One other word of warning about Documents to Go: it was purchased in 2010 by RIM, the company that makes the BlackBerry series of smartphones. When tech companies make these kinds of purchases, they often bring the technology in-house so they can use it solely on their own devices. RIM has made no such decision or announcement about doing the same with Docs to Go, so there is no reason to believe at this time that they will. But who knows what the future will bring? Docs to Go is too good a tool *not* to try; don't let this remote possibility keep you from checking it out.

QuickOffice Connect

QuickOffice is a relative newcomer to the document management arena, and it has been met with mostly good reviews. The app appears to be trying to give users the best of both worlds; the capabilities of Documents to Go, with the user interface of iWork. There's no denying it's a much more pleasant app to work in than Docs to Go.

Like Docs to Go, when you set up QuickOffice you will need to set up your online accounts to access your files—QuickOffice is able to connect to Google Docs, Dropbox, Box.net, MobileMe, Huddle, and SugarSync. You can also use iTunes to sync your files, but now that you are seeing all the great online services that work with these apps, doesn't using iTunes to sync your files seem a bit old-fashioned? Once your services are connected, you can start editing documents.

The QuickOffice feature set is even more basic than Docs to Go— you do not get many options when it comes to editing or formatting text. The PowerPoint functionality is especially disappointing. But QuickOffice has been designed to give a great iPad experience, easily allowing you to drag and drop files directly from the iPad into one of your online accounts, and vice versa. And in that respect, it's a great success.

Office² HD

Office² (as in "Office Squared") is the cheapest of the document management alternatives, but it has most of the same features as those discussed above. Like Docs to Go and QuickOffice, you can sync your documents with the major cloud-based services, including Google Docs, MobileMe, Dropbox, myDisk, iCloud, and Box.net. Unlike the other services above, you cannot edit presentations in Office²—just view them.

Office² offers full-screen text editing, with the same basic Google Docs-like formatting features. Just like the others, you're not going to use Office^2 for hardcore document creation, but instead to make quick edits or create a simple document. I would not rate this app as high as Docs to Go or QuickOffice, but for bargain shoppers, Office^2 may be a good choice.

Other Options

Google Docs—many of the options covered above are able to import your Google Docs into the app so you can edit them as you would any other word processing, spreadsheet, or presentation file. But if you don't want to go to the expense of any of these apps, can you just use Google Docs itself on the iPad? The answer is yes—if you don't mind a *very* primitive document editing experience. To access your Google Docs on the iPad:

- Point your browser to **http://docs.google.com**. A basic listing of your Google Docs will appear.
- To create a new document, press the Create New button in the upper-right corner. On the next screen, select New Spreadsheet or New Document, give your document a title, and press Create. You can then start typing in the new document space.
- To edit an existing document, select it from the document list. Tap Edit in the upper-right corner. A new screen will appear, which will allow you to make edits on the page/spreadsheet.

Let's be clear—this is about as basic as it gets. You will only be able to write text in the document's current font, edit spreadsheets, or add bullet points. You cannot change fonts or styles, add hyperlinks, format text, add images, or use any of the advanced features that the web-based Google Docs offers. Of course, Google updates its software almost every week, so by the time this book is published the functionality may have significantly advanced. But as of the time of printing, don't plan on using Google Docs for anything other than very basic editing of your online documents.

Microsoft Office Web Apps—finally, we come to the giant in the space, and that's Microsoft Office. Unfortunately, the folks in Redmond are woefully behind in the race to make documents available for editing on mobile devices. You can edit Office documents on your Windows Phone 7, if you have one; otherwise, you'll be forced to use **Office Web Apps (http://office.microsoft.com)**. The apps are free to use, but unfortunately you're limited to *view-only access* on your iPad. No editing. No creating new documents. Just viewing. Which makes the Microsoft option your last, among these document management tools.

Actually, that's not *quite* true. There is a way to run a full version of Office on your iPad. It requires you to get into something called **application virtualization**, which will take you much longer than the hour you will be spending reading this book. But if you're still interested in trying it out, you'll need a couple of things: 1) a thin-client app such as **Citrix Receiver for iPad** running on the device; 2) a server-hosted version of Office running in your enterprise data center; and 3) someone from IT to help you connect it up, assuming it will be compatible with your firm or company's network. It is neither cheap nor easy for most IT shops to set this up, which is why it's not a common option for accessing documents on your iPad.

Reading on the iPad

After drafting documents, the activity lawyers probably engage in most often is *reading* those documents. Whether they are reading pleadings or discovery from another party, a deposition of an important witness, the latest case law research, articles from the Internet or important documents for an upcoming transaction, reading is a fundamental part of every lawyer's workday.

And because the iPad was primarily designed as a content *consumption* device, it's extraordinarily well-suited for reading. In this area we'll cover a few of my favorite apps for reading any type of document.

First up are the documents lawyers deal with every day: pleadings, discovery, correspondence, reports, contracts, case law, and others. More often than not, you'll be viewing PDF files, but you also want an app that has the ability to view other document types as well. My two favorite apps for reading documents like these are **GoodReader** and **iAnnotate PDF.**

GoodReader is on everyone's list of top iPad apps, and it's easy to see why. It can handle just about any type of file—Office and iWork documents, PDFs, text files, HTML pages, photos, music and videos. It imports documents using a number of different options, including a temporary Wi-Fi connection, via specific web URL, or by pulling files from mail/FTP servers, Google Docs, Dropbox, Box.net, and iDisk— and we're just getting started!

Once you have loaded GoodReader with the documents you want to read, you'll be dealing with two main views: My Documents and the actual viewing window (see Figure 12).

Within the My Documents screen you'll find a listing of all your documents to the left, with your options for each document to the right. The really powerful part of this screen is found under **Manage Files,** where you can do any number of things:

- Star important documents
- Password-protect sensitive files
- Move documents into folders
- Email documents

Figure 12

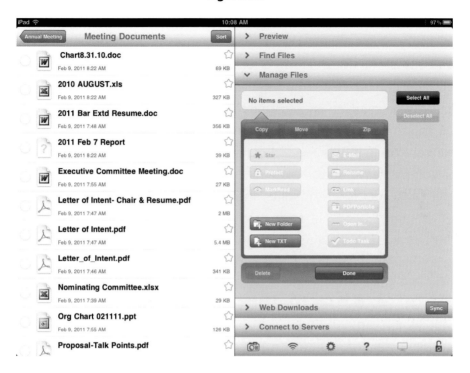

- Create a link to a public copy of the document
- Extract individual documents from a PDF portfolio
- Open the document in other iPad apps that support it
- Create a To Do task (requires the **Appigo Todo** app to be installed on the iPad)
- Create a Zip file of a large number of documents for mailing

And that's not all—the right side of the My Documents screen allows you to preview documents, find files in GoodReader by entering a few keywords, and connect to the online services or web pages you use to download documents.

In the actual document viewing window, you have different options depending on the type of document you're viewing. If you're reading a PDF file, you can change the orientation, crop it, add bookmarks, or even convert the document to a text file (if the PDF supports text extraction). In all views you have the option to send your document to someone by email, to an AirPrint-compatible printer, or to another iPad app that supports it. GoodReader also allows annotations to PDF files: you can highlight, underline, cross out, insert, and replace text, and you can leave notes.

GoodReader is a fast, solid, and dependable app, and should be a part of your iPad app library.

If you need to do some editing on a document, you might choose one of the document management tools above—but if that document is a PDF file, those apps won't work. Instead, you'll want an app that allows you to comment on or otherwise annotate the document. Although GoodReader offers good annotation functionality, in this author's opinion there's no better app for marking up a PDF than **iAnnotate PDF**. If you like to review case law in PDF format, then you'll love this app.

The functionality of iAnnotate PDF is pretty simple, but very powerful. There are a couple of ways to get PDF files into the app. The first is to use the **Aji PDF Service**, a small program that you download to your computer. Just move PDF files into the Aji folder on your desktop, and you can then access those files directly on your iPad. You can also download PDFs directly from certain websites, or by using my favorite option, the ubiquitous Dropbox service.

Once the PDFs you want to read are within iAnnotate, open up a file and start working on it. You'll be presented with two toolbars (see Figures 13 and 14):

Figure 13

Use this toolbar to add bookmarks, navigate from page to page, copy text to a clipboard (if text can be extracted from the PDF), and lock the document.

Here's where the magic really happens. Here you're able to:

- Insert a comment
- Write on the PDF
- Highlight text
- Underline text
- Cross out text

Figure 14

Within no time, you'll be marking up case law, pleadings, or other documents that you need to review. When you're done working on the document, you can move it out of iAnnotate in one of two ways. First, you can simply upload it, either to iTunes or to your Dropbox account. You can also mail, print (using an AirPrint-enabled printer), or open the document in an app that connects up with iAnnotate.

With both GoodReader and iAnnotate, you've got reading and marking up documents down cold. But what about reading articles and pages you find on the Internet? These apps don't really handle web pages that well. That's where **Instapaper** comes in handy. Instapaper is a dead-simple app that makes it easy for you to save long articles or web pages for later reading, without all the annoying ads and extra junk you might find on the average web page (see Figure 15).

Figure 15

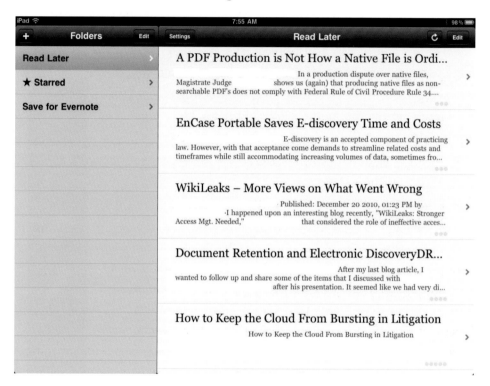

Here's how to get started with Instapaper:
- Head to **www.instapaper.com** and sign up for an account.
- Install the Instapaper app on your iPad. Tap *Settings* and enter the appropriate information under *Your Account* to connect to the online version of Instapaper.
- Still in *Settings*, select *Install "Read Later" in Safari* under *Add Articles*.
- Select *Copy* when prompted.

- Your browser will open with further instructions for installing a "Read Later" bookmark:
    - ▶ First, go to Settings, then Safari, and make sure *Always Show Bookmarks Bar* is turned ON
    - ▶ Back in your browser, bookmark the following page by pressing the + sign, selecting *Add Bookmark*, making sure the bookmark is being saved to the Bookmarks Bar, and then pressing *Save*.
    - ▶ Tap the Bookmarks button in the toolbar, and then tap *Edit*.
    - ▶ Select the *Instapaper: Read Later* bookmark that you just created.
    - ▶ Tap its URL, then tap the X to clear it.
    - ▶ Tap and *hold* your finger in the empty box—when you release your finger, then tap *Paste*. The iPad will paste what we copied a few steps back.
    - ▶ Save your changes and tap *Done*.
    - ▶ You now should have a *Read Later* button on the bookmark bar of your browser.
- Now, when you're reading an article online, you can save it for later simply by pressing the *Read Later* button in your browser.

Once you've added a few articles to your **Read Later** queue, head over to the Instapaper app. You'll see all the articles you've saved, formatted in an easy-to-read layout. After you're done reading, you can do a couple of things with the article: move it to a user-created folder within Instapaper, share it by email, post it to Tumbler or Twitter, read it in GoodReader, print it with an AirPrint-compatible printer, or open it in your browser.

Holding Online Meetings by iPad

If we aren't creating documents and reading them, we lawyers are meeting with people. Those people might be down the hall from us, down the street, or halfway around the world. In the past few years, online meetings have become more and more popular, as the cost of travel has made meeting in person less and less common. Fortunately, several companies are making it easy to conduct and lead meetings from the iPad. Unfortunately, the apps I've used all leave something to be desired, but still have great promise. Here are a few I've found:

- **GoToMeeting**—the terrific GoToMeeting service has an iPad app, but you won't be able to host meetings from it. Right now, all you can do is attend a meeting that was organized online. Once you're in the meeting, the functionality is quite nice; the inability to host your own meeting is a drawback, however.

- **WebEx**—just like GoToMeeting, the WebEx meeting app is pretty cool, once you've entered the meeting. However, you cannot host meetings from this app, either. You *can* schedule and start meetings from the app, if you have a WebEx account.

- **Fuze Meeting**—Fuze Meeting is a relatively new service that's also free, and offers just a bit more functionality in terms of hosting meetings. You need a Fuze account to get started, but once you're registered, you can schedule meetings and invite up to 15 people. Here are a few things you can do within the Fuze app:

  ▶ Once you start your meeting, you'll get a prompt to join the audio conference. You can join directly from your iPad, which will connect you to an audio stream, or you can have Fuze call your phone.

  ▶ You can add content that you want to display at your meeting, but you'd better have it all lined up ahead of time. Currently, you can only add content from your iPad Photo Library, "iPad Document Library" (wherever that is) or Fuze Online Library. So make sure the documents or other items you want to show are preloaded into one of those locations. Then just select them and they'll be added to the queue, and you can begin sharing the content immediately.

▶ Once you are sharing content with other meeting attendees, your options are limited. You can chat with others behind the scenes, or you can use your "iPoint" to point at the item with the digital equivalent of a laser pen.

Needless to say, online meeting tools for the iPad need a little maturation. Attending a meeting is a pleasant experience, but without the ability to host a meeting and show documents, these apps are just not that useful for the average attorney.

Brainstorming, Tablet Style

The last productivity theme we'll cover in this lesson is that of brainstorming. Lawyers do a lot of that—strategizing on the right trial tactics, laying out a plan of action for an upcoming transaction, or just developing a business plan for the law practice. In recent years "mind mapping" software has become a popular way of facilitating the brainstorming process. A mind map is defined by Wikipedia as "a diagram used to represent words, ideas, tasks, or other items, and arranged around a central theme." The iPad has a few good mind mapping apps available, and in this lesson we'll discuss two of them.

MindMeister is a tool I have used on my computer in the past, and I like it quite a bit. It's an offshoot of the mind mapping website (**www.mindmeister.com**), but you don't have to have an account there to use the app. Just click the + sign on the *Maps* screen to start a new map—before you start, you might want to take a look at the sample *My First iPad Map* to see what they look like, and how they are constructed (see Figure 16).

Click the + sign in the upper-right corner to create a new "node," or box that forms part of the map. Click it twice to enter text. In the

Figure 16

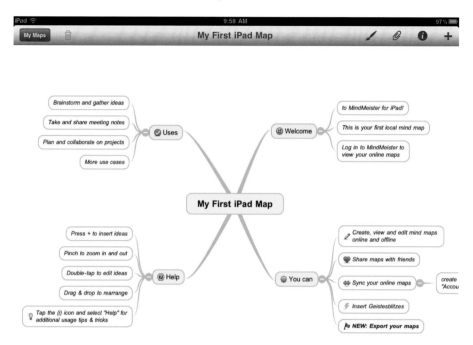

upper-right corner you can access a number of great formatting options by tapping on the paintbrush icon; you can format the text size and color, box shape and color, insert icons, or change the theme of your map.

Once you're done with your map, you can share it in one of several ways. By choosing the *Share this map* option, you can provide others with a link to the map on the MindMeister site. When you press *Export via Mail*, you can choose the format for the map—PDF, PNG, RTF, Freemind, or MindManager file format.

Another interesting mind mapping app is **iThoughts HD**, which appears to have a few more features than MindMeister. First, there are navigation buttons on the top to help you when you are adding new nodes to the map. The formatting features are similar, but it's in the saving and exporting of maps where iThoughts really excels. You can send the map by email, Wi-Fi transfer, to the camera roll on your iPad, or to a cloud-based service like Dropbox, Box.net, or MobileMe. And there are thirteen file formats from which to choose, although most of the formats are handled by different types of proprietary mind map software.

If you like to brainstorm and have never had luck in writing down your ideas, give mind mapping a try. The apps mentioned here, as well as others in the iPad App Store, will make your next brainstorming activity a more pleasurable experience.

Doing Lawyer Things on Your iPad— Legal Apps

So far, we've discussed some of the ways lawyers can use the iPad in their practice. In this Lesson, we'll look at some legal-specific apps, and how lawyers can use them at trial or in doing research. We won't be discussing legal texts in this lesson (except for one); there are just too many of them to mention.

The iPad in the Courtroom

When it comes to lawyers in the courtroom, iPad app developers are so far concentrating on two areas: juries and presentation of evidence. We'll start with the apps pertaining to juries, which have found a terrific case use for a tablet computer. When many lawyers pick a jury, they often do so with a legal pad, diagramming the panel to keep track of who is who, and who said what. This is where **iJuror** comes in handy. It appears to be geared primarily to juries in criminal trials, but it can still be used to select a jury in other cases (see Figure 17).

The graphical layout of iJuror allows you to enter information for each juror, including name, employer, hometown, and more demographic data like age, sex, race, marital status, children, education, police in the family, prior arrests, whether the person has been victim-

Figure 17

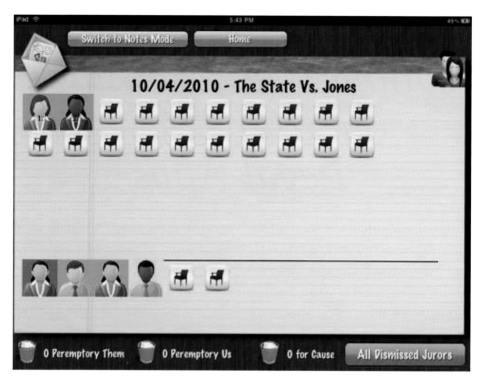

ized by crime (or perhaps was a prior Plaintiff), and any prior jury experience. Once you've entered the information, you can then just drag and drop the panelists to choose jurors or alternates, or dismiss them, and indicate the reason for their dismissal.

The primary benefit of iJuror is that it gives you a clean layout of your jury panel. It does not allow you to create your own variables of the information that may be of greater value to you for the case in question, nor will you be able to "score" jurors on any scale that is a true benefit of your typical computer-based voir dire program.

Jury Duty is another jury selection app that you may need to complete *before* you come into the courtroom, because a lot of data entry is required. You can enter information on each jury panelist, with preselected information and a number of optional fields. You can also create a list of topics you want to cover with each juror, and can track these topics as "discussed" or "not discussed" on the individual panelist page. Once all juror information is entered, you can put together the Seating Chart, and drag and drop assigned jurors to any seat. You can then indicate whether the panelist was accepted, rejected, struck for cause, or gave a positive or negative impression. There's also a handy notes field to record any thoughts you might have on the panelist.

In contrast, **Jury Tracker** is really designed to deal with your jury *after* they have been selected. It captures the reactions of jurors throughout the trial. Once you have entered information on all of the jurors, each will have their own screen for you (or a paralegal or assistant, more likely) to record their reactions throughout the trial. You can record facial reactions (nodding, shaking head, crying, smiling) as well as body motions (looking at watch, bored, taking notes). You can also refine these reactions, and designate jurors as "leaders" or "followers," plaintiff or defendant-oriented, or as a "key" juror (see Figure 18).

Once this data is entered into the app, you can then run reports for each juror or the panel as a whole. Reports can be filtered to show general reactions over the course of the day or for a particular witness, to see who is leaning for the plaintiff or defendant, or those with positive vs. negative body language. These reports can be saved and emailed to others on the trial team, if desired.

A major drawback of Jury Tracker is that information can only be entered for one juror at a time; if multiple jurors react to testimony at the same time, it will be cumbersome to move back and forth between juror screens to record their reactions. You'll also need someone to enter the data for you, most likely a paralegal or assistant who is there solely to observe the jury and enter the information—it would be a full-time job, but would likely cost less than hiring a jury consultant to sit in court all day and do many of the same things.

Figure 18

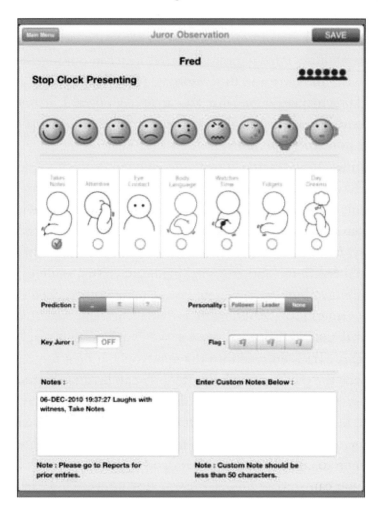

As these trial apps mature, it will be interesting to see if they integrate with others, as with the document management apps. It would be nice to pick your jury using iJuror, then take all the information on the final jury panel and send it automatically to Jury Tracker. Instead, you're currently stuck with reentering all of that information, if you plan to use both apps at trial.

Once the trial is started, you'll need technology to present your evidence to the jury. There are two apps currently available to help with this, although both have pretty distinct limitations, at least at the time of this book's publication. There are several excellent trial presentation programs you can use to display evidence at trial, including Sanction and Trial Director; neither of the iPad apps mentioned below have the powerful features of those two programs. However, the apps *do* have uses in the courtroom, under the right circumstances and at the right trials, hearings or even depositions.

The first app is **TrialPad**. Setting up a case in TrialPad is easy—simply select the + sign on the home screen, and a new folder will pop up that you can name and give a description. Then it's time to add your documents. As this is being written, TrialPad only supports PDF files, so you will need to make sure everything is converted to PDF before you use this app. You can only add the files in two ways: using File Sharing in iTunes (*See Lesson 4*), or by email. On the iPad, press and hold the PDF email attachment, and one of your options will be *Open in "TrialPad."* TrialPad promises to add Dropbox integration in future releases, which would definitely improve the ability to add documents.

You can organize documents by file or by folder on the left side of the screen; just press the + sign at the bottom to add a folder. According to some, TrialPad will not handle very large PDF files, which can cause the app to crash. Once you have your documents loaded into TrialPad, you can start organizing them, moving them into different folders by issue, witness, or other criteria. You can also mark a document as "Hot" by pressing the flaming button in the upper-right corner. Then you can easily access all Hot Docs in a particular case by pressing the Hot Docs button in the File Manager.

TrialPad offers three basic annotation tools—highlight, red pen, and redact. You can use any of these options to mark up your exhibits either ahead of time, or during presentation at trial or hearing. You'll need to keep pressing the buttons after every time you use one of the tools—it returns to its default "zoom" state after each use.

When you are ready to present the document, make sure you've attached a VGA cable to your iPad, attach the cable to a projector, then move the **Output** button from **Off** to **On**. You'll see a Go, Pause, and Stop button at the bottom of the screen, which you can use to move through your documents. Pause allows you to select another document without displaying it on the screen—when you're ready to show that document, press Go and the document is visible. After you're done with the document, press Stop to clear the screen.

The other trial presentation app, **Evidence**, supports more file types than TrialPad, including JPG, PNG and TIFF images, as well as PowerPoint and text files. However, multipage TIFFs, which are routinely used in the more robust trial presentation programs, are not supported here; you cannot move past the first page of the TIFF. At the time of this book's publication, documents can be added to Evidence only through File Sharing in iTunes.

Documents are handled a bit differently by Evidence—there are no folders, so you cannot organize documents for a particular case, and there's no way to reorder the exhibits in the database. For annotating documents, Evidence has a highlight and underlining/circling tool, but no redaction feature. The presentation mode is also somewhat different, in that you only have one button—Publish—to present documents. If you want to move to another exhibit, you'll need to press the Publish button again, once to clear the current document, another to bring up the next one.

A significant drawback of Evidence is the inability to display a full page of a document—it will only display partial pages. Many times you need to show a judge or jury the full document, even though they may not be able to read all of the text on it without zooming in.

Neither TrialPad nor Evidence comes remotely close to the power of a Sanction or Trial Director, but if you only need to present a few files in a small case or to a judge at a hearing, you probably don't need all the bells and whistles. These apps, limitations notwithstanding, should work just fine in small matters.

Back at the Office, or Anywhere Else—Legal Research

I could make this a much longer book going through the hundreds of iPad apps designed to provide access to state statutes, codes and rules of procedure. If you are interested in carrying a full library of laws, rules, and regulations on your iPad, just head over to the iTunes store and do a search under "law" or "legal."

In this section, however, I want to highlight two apps that are undeniably helpful to any lawyer, no matter where you happen to be located. The first is **Fastcase**, the iPad companion to the online service. The iPad app is free to use, which means that you won't be getting as many features as you might if you signed up for a paid subscription. That said, the research features are still quite nice.

To start, select New Search and enter your search terms. Federal cases (Circuit, District and Bankruptcy) are available, as well as case law from all 50 states. You can filter your search by Jurisdiction and Date Range, and you can choose to have your results check Authorities for cases citing and cited by a particular case. You can go through your results and save them to a Saved Documents area. That's about all you can do with the free version.

If you upgrade to the "Premium" edition of Fastcase, you get a number of useful features, including:
- Unlimited customer support
- Dual-column printing of documents

- More powerful sorting tools
- The ability to email a case or search results
- Visual maps of search results
- Access to more libraries, such as court rules, administrative regulations and constitutions
- Newspaper search, people finder, business intelligence, and forms
- Unified search within PACER (one search for all courts)

To get all of this, you'll have to subscribe to one of the Fastcase services, which at the time of this book's publication was between $65-$95/month, depending on the plan you choose. But for fast, mobile legal research, the free version is a great app, as long as you understand the limitations.

One last legal app, and that's **Black's Law Dictionary**. All you'll get is the dictionary, and it's not cheap—but cheaper than the printed version. But it's Black's Law Dictionary—something every lawyer needs and uses in their practice at some point. It's definitely worth the 50 bucks or so to have it available on your iPad whenever you need a legal definition.

Every month thousands of new apps for the iPad roll out, and more and more of them are law-related apps. Make sure to check back regularly at **http://www.tommighell.com/ipad** to read the latest about iPad apps for lawyers.

The Ever-Changing Nature of Technology: The Next Generation of iPad

The challenge of writing a book about technology is that it's always changing—the technology, that is. Indeed, although as I finish the final draft of this book I am using the first-generation iPad, the newest iPad, dubbed "iPad 2," will have been released by Apple by the time this book is published.

The iPad 2 comes with some great new features, including front and rear-facing cameras, faster graphics, all in a thinner, redesigned chassis. The good news is that the improvements in iPad 2 do not affect the basic functionality of the device. In other words, what you have learned in this book should apply to any iPad you own, whether it's a first or second-generation device.

While the iPad's hardware only gets updated once a year, the apps that run on the device are being updated constantly by their developers, and features come and go with sometimes dizzying frequency. The features described for certain apps I mention here may not be available by the time you read this book, and new features may have debuted that take care of particular issues I mentioned concerning the app. In other words, *your mileage may vary*. I'm creating a website at **http://www.tommighell.com/ipad,** where I'll post the latest on iPad (and other tablet) apps for lawyers; so check there regularly for information as it gets updated.

Configuring Security Settings

When you first set up your iPad (*see Introduction: Getting Started*), one of the first things you want to do is make sure your security settings are properly configured. Unfortunately, it's very easy to leave an iPad on a plane, in a taxi, or in your hotel room, and computing devices are always in danger of being stolen. To configure the security options, press *Settings*, then *General*, then *Passcode Lock*.

- **Simple Passcode**—by default, this is switched ON, to allow you to configure a 4-digit passcode. If you want a more secure passcode, move this setting to OFF, and follow the instructions below.

- **Turn Passcode On**—press this button next, and you'll be prompted to enter a passcode. If *Simple Passcode* below is in the ON position, it will be a 4-digit passcode. If you turned *Simple Passcode* to the OFF position, you can enter a passcode of any length. Enter your passcode once, then enter it again for confirmation. Now your passcode is set.

- **Require Passcode**—this option will require you to enter your passcode after the iPad has been idle for a certain period of time. You can set this option for Immediately, 1 minute, 5 minutes, or 15 minutes. I recommend 1 minute, for maximum security without having you constantly entering the passcode.

- **Erase Data**—when turned ON, this option will erase all data on your iPad after ten failed attempts at entering the passcode. I recommend you turn this option ON.

If your iPad does end up lost or stolen, you can still protect it from afar. Find a friend with an iPhone or iPad (or use your own iPhone, if you have one), visit the App Store and download the free **Find My iPhone** app. Once installed, log in to your Apple account, and the app will display a map showing where your iPad happens to be at that very moment. Of course, the iPad will need to be on and connected to the Internet, which means you may need to try several times before you can actually locate the device. Once you do, you have a couple of options: you can make it play a sound, if the iPad happens to be nearby; you can lock it, so that a passcode must be used to access it again; or you can erase all the data on it.

A few other smart security options include:

- When you back up your data in iTunes, you have the option of encrypting your data. When your iPad is connected to iTunes, click on the *Summary* tab and scroll to *Options* at the bottom. Check the *Encrypt iPad backup* option, and then set (or change) your password.
- Consider using a VPN, or Virtual Private Network, that provides a secure connection when you are using the device. To enable a VPN, press *Settings*, then *Network*, then *VPN*. There are also apps, like **AnyConnect**, that can set up a VPN for you; just search for "VPN" in the App Store.
- Disable Bluetooth—if you're not using your Bluetooth connection, make sure it's turned off. Press *Settings*, then *General*, then *Bluetooth*.
- If you want to enable security settings for the Safari browser, press *Settings*, then *Safari*.
  - ▶ *Fraud Warning*—move to ON
  - ▶ *Block Pop-Ups*—move to ON
  - ▶ *Clear History, Cookies, Cache*—it's a good idea to periodically clear your browser of these items

Finger Moves and Shortcuts

Finger Moves

The iPad makes use of several different finger moves to accomplish certain tasks. Here are the main finger moves, and what each does:

- **Tap.** With the tip of your finger, directly touch what you see on screen—it can be an icon, song title, or app control. You don't need to push hard—a gentle press is all it takes.
- **Drag.** Keep your finger pressed on the screen, and slide it around to scroll to different parts of the screen. This move helps you set volume sliders or pan around objects larger than the screen. You can also try out the "two-finger drag" to scroll a window within another window.
- **Slide.** Almost like a drag, but you're only going to use the Slide in one instance; to interact with the iPad's Unlock/Confirm button, which is where you wake your iPad or confirm a shut-down of the device.
- **Flick.** By lightly whipping your finger up or down the screen, you can watch the web page, song list, or other long page zip by in the direction of your flick.
- **Finger Spread and Pinch.** To zoom into a part of a page or picture, take your thumb and index finger, put them on the screen where you want to zoom, and spread them out across the glass.

To zoom out, do the same thing, but this time pinch your thumb and index finger together.

- **Double Tap.** In some apps it's an easy way to quickly zoom into something. In videos it can be used to toggle between full-screen and widescreen view.

Shortcuts

Cut, Copy and Paste—you'll get all of these commands in the same menu.

- First, double-tap the word or sentence you want to cut or copy. A Cut | Copy | Paste box pops up.
- A blue scroll bar will appear, with dots on each end; to select more words, sentences, or a whole paragraph, use the dots on each end to expand your selection.
  - ▶ For pages you can't edit, you'll need to hold your finger down until a magnifying glass and cursor appears. Drag the cursor to the text you want to copy.
  - ▶ When you lift your finger, the Select | Select All box appears. Select gives you the blue dots so you can highlight all the text you want to copy, while Select All highlights everything onscreen.
  - ▶ After you have selected your text, lift your finger, and a Copy button will appear.
  - ▶ If you want to select a whole paragraph at once, tap it quickly four times.
- Tap the Cut or Copy command (depending on the box you see).
- Tap the spot where you want to paste the text or photo. A Paste button will pop up.
- Tap the Paste button to insert the text or photo into its new location.

Web Browser Shortcuts—when you're working in the Safari browser on your iPad, the keyboard helps you out with some keys for commonly-used web language.

- When typing a URL in the address bar, the keyboard helpfully gives you a slash, hyphen, and an underscore.
- You also get a .com button to complete the web address.
- If you're going to a domain other than .com, simply press and hold the .com button, and you'll get a choice of .net, org, .us, and .edu. Just slide your finger to the right extension and let go.

Keyboard Shortcuts

- Need an accent on that e, or other letter? Press and hold the letter you are typing (e, u, i, o, a, or n), and you'll see a number of different choices for that letter.
- You can also force keys to appear on the main keyboard that aren't originally there. For example, to get to an apostrophe or quotation mark, you typically have to press the .?123 key to tap those keys. But if you just press down the comma (,) button and slide, you'll see the apostrophe appear above. Try the same thing with the period (.) button, and quotation marks will appear.
- The iPad's AutoCorrect feature is both a blessing and a curse. It will automatically correct your bad typing, which can be great. But if you're not paying attention, it can also substitute a completely different word for what you originally intended. Here are two tips for dealing with AutoCorrect:
  - ▶ As you are typing a word, AutoCorrect may pop up an alternate suggestion. If that's the word you want, simply hit the Space bar and keep going—the word will be automatically accepted. If you don't like the suggested correction, just tap it to make it go away.

▶ If you don't look at the text when you type, you might miss words as they are AutoCorrected. To prevent this, go to **Settings→ General→Accessibility→Speak Auto-Text**. From now on, your iPad will speak when it makes an AutoCorrect suggestion.

■ Go to **Settings→General→Keyboard** to turn other shortcuts on or off:

▶ Auto-Capitalization—will automatically capitalize the first letter after a period.

▶ Enable Caps Lock—When you double-tap the Shift key, it turns blue and you can type in ALL CAPS until you tap Shift again to turn it off.

▶ "." Shortcut—if you turn this on, every time you double tap the space bar the iPad will insert a period followed by a space.

Advanced Email Options

In *Lesson 2*, I covered the basics of setting up your email, calendar and contacts. But there are many more options available to configure email on your iPad, and they could definitely use a little explanation. Here's a brief description of the other options you have under the *Mail, Contacts, Calendars* view in *Settings*.

If you use email from a service other than Exchange, Gmail, Yahoo, AOL, or MobileMe, you can set it up under the *Other* option when you add an email account. To get there, go to *Settings*, then *Mail, Contacts, Calendars*, then *Add Account*. Press the *Other* button to get started.

- **Mail: Add Mail Account**—Press this button to add an email account from a service other than the ones covered above. You'll be entering your *Name, Email Address, Password*, and *Description* (Optional).

- **Contacts: Add LDAP Account**—If your firm or office uses an *LDAP* (Lightweight Directory Access Protocol) server, press this button and add your *User Name, Password, Description* (optional), and the LDAP *Server Name*.

- **Contacts: Add CardDAV Account**—CardDAV is an address book client designed to allow users to access and share contact data on a server. If you want to add your CardDAV contacts, press this button and add your *User Name, Password, Description* (optional), and the CardDAV *Server Name*.

- **Calendar: Add CalDAV Account**—a CalDAV account is similar to the CardDAV account, but for your calendar items. If you use a CalDAV account, press this button and add your *User Name, Password, Description* (Optional), and the CalDAV *Server Name*.
- **Calendar: Add Subscribed Calendar**—a "Subscribed Calendar" is a calendar with the *.ics* (or Internet Connection Sharing) extension. It allows users to connect to calendars across the Internet without using one of the mail services described above. For example, the TripIt travel service allows you to subscribe to an iCalendar feed of all your upcoming travel plans. To add an iCal subscription to your iPad, just press this option and enter the *Server* or subscription address.

The iPad also allows you to set up your Mail, Contacts and Calendar through iTunes itself. With your iPad plugged in to your computer, click on your device in the left menu bar of iTunes to see the specific options for the iPad (see Figure 19).

Figure 19

Click on Info. You'll see options for syncing your Contacts, Calendar and Mail to the iPad. Curiously, you don't get as many options here as within the iPad's settings itself; you only get the following options:

- Contacts—Outlook, Google Contacts, Windows Contacts, and Yahoo! Address Book
- Calendar—Outlook only
- Mail—Outlook and Windows mail only
- Bookmarks—Internet Explorer only
- Notes—Outlook only

One specific benefit of using iTunes to configure these options is that you can identify specific groups of contacts, individual calendars, or particular email accounts you want to sync. You don't get that kind of power with the iPad's internal settings.

Once you have set up your email account, go back to the *Mail, Contacts, Calendars* main page to configure additional options (see Figure 20).

- **Fetch New Data**—You can choose to either "Push" or "Fetch" new email messages. "Push" means that a connection is opened whenever a message is available to deliver. "Fetch" opens a connection at specific, pre-defined intervals—in the case of the iPad every 15 minutes, 30 minutes, hourly, or you can elect a Manual fetch. If you press the *Advanced* button, you can configure Push/Fetch options for each individual account you have— although some accounts may not have Push options available.
- **Mail: Show**—you may not need to show all of the email in a folder when reviewing it. This option allows you to choose whether the iPad displays the most recent 25, 50, 75, 100, or 200 messages.
- **Mail: Preview**—use this option to specify how many lines of type appear as a "preview" of your email—1, 2, 3, 4, 5, or no lines at all.

Figure 20

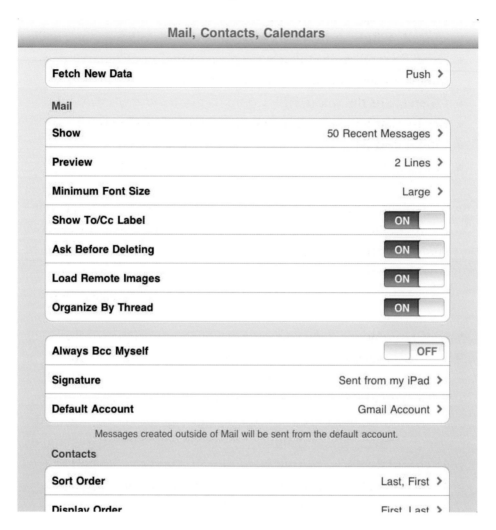

Mail, Contacts, Calendars

Fetch New Data	Push >

Mail

Show	50 Recent Messages >
Preview	2 Lines >
Minimum Font Size	Large >
Show To/Cc Label	ON
Ask Before Deleting	ON
Load Remote Images	ON
Organize By Thread	ON

Always Bcc Myself	OFF
Signature	Sent from my iPad >
Default Account	Gmail Account >

Messages created outside of Mail will be sent from the default account.

Contacts

Sort Order	Last, First >
Display Order	First, Last >

- **Mail: Minimum Font Size**—what font size do you want to use to read your email? The iPad gives you five choices: Small, Medium, Large, Extra Large, and Giant.
- **Mail: Show to/Cc Label**—this option will display a small "To" or "Cc" label on each email in the left mail list (in landscape

view), to denote whether you are the primary recipient or are simply being copied on the message.

■ **Mail: Ask Before Deleting**—if you leave this option ON, you'll see a "Delete" button that you must press to confirm each deletion of a message. Otherwise, the email will be deleted with a simple swipe of the finger. This option is good to have if you have fingers that tend to accidentally delete the wrong message.

■ **Mail: Load Remote Images**—if your email messages have images in them, pressing ON for this option will allow the images to be downloaded and viewed in your email.

■ **Mail: Organize by Thread**—this option allows you to view the entire thread of an email conversation at once. Instead of being spread out throughout a long list of email messages, a threaded conversation stays together. When you press on that email message, you'll get a sublisting with all of the other messages in the conversation.

■ **Mail: Always Bcc Myself**—if you like to keep copies of the email you send, select this option—it will insert your email address into the Bcc field of all messages you compose.

■ **Mail: Signature**—here you can specify the signature you want to appear at the bottom of every message. The default message is "Sent from my iPad," which you may want to change if you are using the iPad for business purposes.

■ **Mail: Default Account**—if you have multiple email accounts configured, the iPad will require that one account be designated the "Default," for all messages created outside of Mail. For example, if you try to mail a news article from apps like Google Reader or Instapaper, the message will be sent from your Default Account.

■ **Contacts: Sort Order**—Specify how you want your Contacts sorted—First Name/Last Name, or Last Name/First Name.

- **Contacts: Display Order**—specify here how you want your Contacts displayed, with the same options.
- **Contacts: Default Account**—as with email, you must select a default account where newly created contacts will be added.
- **Calendars: New Invitation Alerts**—want to be alerted of new calendar items as they are delivered to you? Leave this option ON.
- **Calendars: Sync**—to save space on your calendar, this option allows you to specify how far back events should be included on your iPad. Your options are 2 Weeks Back, 1 Month Back, 3 Months Back, 6 Months Back, or All Events
- **Calendars: Time Zone Support**—If you select ON, event days will display the time zone you have selected for your calendars. If you select OFF, the events will display according to the time zone of your current location.

Best Apps for Lawyers

The following is a nonexclusive, nonexhaustive listing of iPad apps that lawyers will find useful, interesting, or fun. This listing will be posted and continuously updated at **http://www.tommighell.com/ipad**.

But first, a few words about using the iPad App Store. Apps are the life blood of your iPad, and the App Store is where you can get a blood transfusion. You can download apps in two ways: 1) directly in iTunes; or 2) through the App Store icon on your iPad. We'll use the iPad App Store for purposes of our discussion (see Figure 21).

Figure 21

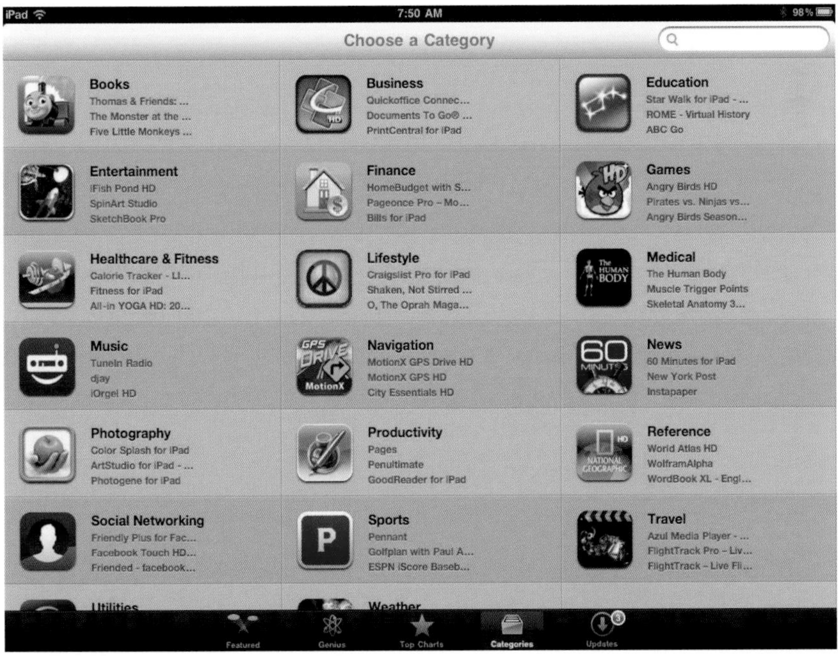

Across the bottom of the screen you have five options:
- **Featured**—special apps highlighted by the App Store
- **Genius**—suggestions for apps that are similar to other apps already on your iPad
- **Top Charts**—the most popular Paid and Free apps in the App Store
- **Categories**—browse the App Store for a particular type of app
- **Updates**—here you'll find a list of apps already on your iPad with updated versions ready to download

Use one of these buttons to start looking for apps. You can also use the Search Box (in the upper right-hand corner) to enter keywords that will help you search for apps. When you find one you like, press on the price tag (or the Free button, if it's free). Enter your iTunes password, and the app will automatically be downloaded and installed. (if the app is too big to install over a wireless or 3G connection, iTunes will tell you to download the app using the iTunes account on your computer).

If you get tired of an app and are ready to get rid of it, there are again two ways to do it—within the iPad or in iTunes.
- To delete an app from your iPad, just press and hold the icon until it begins to jiggle. Press the X in the left corner, and you'll be prompted to confirm the deletion.
- Within iTunes, connect your iPad and then navigate to it in the left-hand menu. Click the Apps tab, and uncheck the boxes next to the apps you don't want. They will be removed on the next sync. To remove an app permanently from your computer, then right-click on it and select Delete.

Productivity
- iAnnotate
- Elements

- PlainText
- Writer
- Evernote
- Documents to Go
- Pages
- Numbers
- Keynote
- QuickOffice Mobile Connect Suite
- Teleprompt+ for iPad
- Instapaper
- Others
  - ▶ Helvitenote
  - ▶ CourseNotes
  - ▶ Notebooks for iPad
  - ▶ Audiotorium
  - ▶ Notability
  - ▶ Simplenote
- Dragon Dictate

Email Apps

- Lotus Notes Traveler App
- GW Mail—Groupwise

To Do and Task Management

- Todo for iPad
- Task Pro
- Toodledo
- OmniFocus
- Things for iPad

Databases

- Bento for iPad
- HanDBase for iPad
- FileMaker Go for iPad
- SQLTouch

Mind-Mapping

- iThoughts HD
- MindNote
- Instaviz
- Whiteboard HD

Conferencing and Meetings

- WebEx
- GoToMeeting
- Fuze Meeting

Law-Specific

- Black's Law Dictionary
- Fastcase
- JuryTracker
- Jury Duty
- iJuror
- TrialPad
- Evidence

File and Document Management

- GoodReader
- Dropbox
- Box.net
- MobileMe

- Air Sharing HD
- ReaddleDocs
- FileApp Pro
- PrintCentral for iPad
- Print N Share
- Print Magic HD
- Printer Pro

Remote Access

- Citrix Receiver for iPad
- PocketCloud
- LogMeIn Ignition
- Mocha VNC
- Connect My PC

Utilities

- ZipThat
- Calculator Pro
- Alarm Clock HD Pro

Fun

- Wallpaper apps
- Angry Birds
- Twitter
- Tweetdeck
- Friendly
- Flipboard
- iTeleport
- Trapster
- Zosh
- Air Sketch

Index

Selected Books from . . .
THE ABA LAW PRACTICE MANAGEMENT SECTION

The Lawyer's Guide to Microsoft Word 2007
By Ben M. Schorr
Microsoft Word is one of the most used applications in the Microsoft Office suite—there are few applications more fundamental than putting words on paper. Most lawyers use Word and few of them get everything they can from it. Because the documents you create are complex and important—your law practice depends, to some degree, upon the quality of the documents you produce and the efficiency with which you can produce them. Focusing on the tools and features that are essential for lawyers in their everyday practice, *The Lawyer's Guide to Microsoft Word* explains in detail the key components to help make you more effective, more efficient and more successful.

The Lawyer's Guide to Marketing on the Internet, Third Edition
By Gregory H. Siskind, Deborah McMurray, and Richard P. Klau
In today's competitive environment, it is critical to have a comprehensive online marketing strategy that uses all the tools possible to differentiate your firm and gain new clients. The Lawyer's Guide to Marketing on the Internet, in a completely updated and revised third edition, showcases practical online strategies and the latest innovations so that you can immediately participate in decisions about your firm's Web marketing effort. With advice that can be implemented by established and young practices alike, this comprehensive guide will be a crucial component to streamlining your marketing efforts.

The Lawyer's Guide to Adobe Acrobat, Third Edition
By David L. Masters
This book was written to help lawyers increase productivity, decrease costs, and improve client services by moving from paper-based files to digital records. This updated and revised edition focuses on the ways lawyers can benefit from using the most current software, Adobe® Acrobat 8, to create Portable Document Format (PDF) files.

PDF files are reliable, easy-to-use, electronic files for sharing, reviewing, filing, and archiving documents across diverse applications, business processes, and platforms. The format is so reliable that the federal courts' Case Management/Electronic Case Files (CM/ECF) program and state courts that use Lexis-Nexis File & Serve have settled on PDF as the standard.

You'll learn how to:

* Create PDF files from a number of programs, including Microsoft Office
* Use PDF files the smart way
* Markup text and add comments
* Digitally, and securely, sign documents
* Extract content from PDF files
* Create electronic briefs and forms

The Electronic Evidence and Discovery Handbook: Forms, Checklists, and Guidelines
By Sharon D. Nelson, Bruce A. Olson, and John W. Simek
The use of electronic evidence has increased dramatically over the past few years, but many lawyers still struggle with the complexities of electronic discovery. This substantial book provides lawyers with the templates they need to frame their discovery requests and provides helpful advice on what they can subpoena. In addition to the ready-made forms, the authors also supply explanations to bring you up to speed on the electronic discovery field. The accompanying CD-ROM features over 70 forms, including, Motions for Protective Orders, Preservation and Spoliation Documents, Motions to Compel, Electronic Evidence Protocol Agreements, Requests for Production, Internet Services Agreements, and more. Also included is a full electronic evidence case digest with over 300 cases detailed!

The 2011 Solo and Small Firm Legal Technology Guide
By Sharon D. Nelson, John W. Simek, and Michael C. Maschke
This annual guide is the only one of its kind written to help solo and small firm lawyers find the best technology for their dollar. You'll find the most current information and recommendations on computers, servers, networking equipment, legal software, printers, security products, smartphones, the iPad and anything else a law office might need. It's written in clear, easily understandable language to make implementation simpler if you choose to do it yourself, or you can use it in conjunction with your IT consultant.

Social Media for Lawyers: The Next Frontier
By Carolyn Elefant and Nicole Black
The world of legal marketing has changed with the rise of social media sites such as Linkedin, Twitter, and Facebook. Law firms are seeking their companies attention with tweets, videos, blog posts, pictures, and online content. Social media is fast and delivers news at record pace. This book provides you with a practical, goal-centric approach to using social media in your law practice that will enable you to identify social media platforms and tools that fit your practice and implement them easily, efficiently, and ethically.

How to Start and Build a Law Practice, Fifth Edition
By Jay G Foonberg
This classic ABA bestseller has been used by tens of thousands of lawyers as the comprehensive guide to planning, launching, and growing a successful practice. It's packed with over 600 pages of guidance on identifying the right location, finding clients, setting fees, managing your office, maintaining an ethical and responsible practice, maximizing available resources, upholding your standards, and much more. If you're committed to starting your own practice, this book will give you the expert advice you need to make it succeed.

Google for Lawyers: Essential Search Tips and Productivity Tools
By Carole A. Levitt and Mark E. Rosch
This book introduces novice Internet searchers to the diverse collection of information locatable through Google. The book discusses the importance of including effective Google searching as part of a lawyer's due diligence, and cites case law that mandates that lawyers should use Google and other resources available on the Internet, where applicable. For intermediate and advanced users, the book unlocks the power of various advanced search strategies and hidden search features they might not be aware of.

Find Info Like a Pro, Volume 1: Mining the Internet's Publicly Available Resources for Investigative Research
By Carole A. Levitt and Mark E. Rosch
This complete hands-on guide shares the secrets, shortcuts, and realities of conducting investigative and background research using the sources of publicly available information available on the Internet. Written for legal professionals, this comprehensive desk book lists, categorizes, and describes hundreds of free and fee-based Internet sites. The resources and techniques in this book are useful for investigations; depositions; locating missing witnesses, clients, or heirs; and trial preparation, among other research challenges facing legal professionals. In addition, a CD-ROM is included, which features clickable links to all of the sites contained in the book.

Find Info Like a Pro, Volume 2: Mining the Internet's Public Records for Investigative Research
By Carole A. Levitt and Mark E. Rosch
Don't waste time and money on hiring someone to do your investigative research when you can do it yourself. The second volume in this important series focuses on public records that are filed and stored with government agencies, which are accessible for public inspection. The authors address both paid and unpaid resources on the Internet.

The Lawyer's Guide to Microsoft Outlook 2007
By Ben M. Schorr
Outlook is the most used application in Microsoft Office, but are you using it to your greatest advantage? *The Lawyer's Guide to Microsoft Outlook 2007* is the only guide written specifically for lawyers to help you be more productive, more efficient and more successful. More than just email, Outlook is also a powerful task, contact, and scheduling manager that will improve your practice. From helping you log and track phone calls, meetings, and correspondence to archiving closed case material in one easy-to-store location, this book unlocks the secrets of "underappreciated" features that you will use every day. Written in plain language by a twenty-year veteran of law office technol-ogy and ABA member, you'll find:

- Tips and tricks to effectively transfer information between all components of the software
- The eight new features in Outlook 2007 that lawyers will love
- A tour of major product features and how lawyers can best use them
- Mistakes lawyers should avoid when using Outlook
- What to do when you're away from the office

The Lawyer's Guide to Microsoft Excel 2007
By John C. Tredennick
Did you know Excel can help you analyze and present your cases more effectively or help you better understand and manage complex business transactions? Designed as a hands-on manual for beginners as well as longtime spreadsheet users, you'll learn how to build spreadsheets from scratch, use them to analyze issues, and to create graphics presentation. Key lessons include:

- Spreadsheets 101: How to get started for beginners
- Advanced Spreadsheets: How to use formulas to calculate values for settlement offers, and damages, business deals
- Simple Graphics and Charts: How to make sophisticated charts for the court or to impress your clients
- Sorting and filtering data and more

Virtual Law Practice: How to Deliver Legal Services Online
By Stephanie L. Kimbro
The legal market has recently experienced a dramatic shift as lawyers seek out alternative methods of practicing law and providing more affordable legal services. Virtual law practice is revolutionizing the way the public receives legal services and how legal professionals work with clients. If you are interested in this form of practicing law, *Virtual Law Practice* will help you:

- Responsibly deliver legal services online to your clients
- Successfully set up and operate a virtual law office
- Establish a virtual law practice online through a secure, client-specific portal
- Manage and market your virtual law practice
- Understand state ethics and advisory opinions
- Find more flexibility and work/life balance in the legal profession

The Lawyer's Guide to LexisNexis CaseMap
By Daniel J. Siegel
LexisNexis CaseMap is a computer program that makes analyzing cases easier and allows lawyers to do a better job for their clients in less time. Many consider this an essential law office tool. If you are interested in learning more about LexisNexis CaseMap, this book will help you:

- Analyze the strengths and weaknesses of your cases quickly and easily;
- Learn how to create files for people, organizations and issues, while avoiding duplication;
- Customize CaseMap so that you can get the most out of your data;
- Enter data so that you can easily prepare for trial, hearings, depositions, and motions for summary judgment;
- Import data from a wide range of programs, including Microsoft Outlook;
- Understand CaseMap's many Reports and ReportBooks;
- Use the Adobe DocPreviewer to import PDFs and quickly create facts and objects; and
- Learn how to perform advanced searches plus how to save and update your results.

30-Day Risk-Free Order Form
Call Today! 1-800-285-2221
Monday–Friday, 7:30 AM – 5:30 PM, Central Time

Qty	Title	LPM Price	Regular Price	Total
_____	The Lawyer's Guide to Microsoft Word 2007 (5110697)	$49.95	$ 69.95	$_____
_____	The Lawyer's Guide to Marketing on the Internet, Third Edition (5110585)	74.95	84.95	$_____
_____	The Lawyer's Guide to Adobe Acrobat, Third Edition (5110588)	49.95	79.95	$_____
_____	The Electronic Evidence and Discovery Handbook: Forms, Checklists, and Guidelines (5110569)	99.95	129.95	$_____
_____	The 2011 Solo and Small Firm Legal Technology Guide (5110716)	54.95	89.95	$_____
_____	Social Media for Lawyers: The Next Frontier (5110710)	47.95	79.95	$_____
_____	How to Start and Build a Law Practice, Fifth Edition (5110508)	57.95	69.95	$_____
_____	Google for Lawyers: Essential Search Tips and Productivity Tools (5110704)	47.95	79.95	$_____
_____	Find Info Like a Pro, Volume 1: Mining the Internet's Publicly Available Resources for Investigative Research (5110708)	47.95	79.95	$_____
_____	Find Info Like a Pro, Volume 2: Mining the Internet's Public Records for Investigative Research (5110709)	47.95	79.95	$_____
_____	The Lawyer's Guide to Microsoft Outlook 2007 (5110661)	49.99	69.99	$_____
_____	The Lawyer's Guide to Microsoft Excel 2007 (5110665)	49.95	69.95	$_____
_____	Virtual Law Practice: How to Deliver Legal Services Online (5110707)	47.95	79.95	$_____
_____	The Lawyer's Guide to LexisNexis CaseMap (5110715)	47.95	79.95	$_____

*Postage and Handling	
$10.00 to $49.99	$5.95
$50.00 to $99.99	$7.95
$100.00 to $199.99	$9.95
$200.00+	$12.95

**Tax	
DC residents add 6%	
IL residents add 9.75%	

*Postage and Handling	$_____
**Tax	$_____
TOTAL	$_____

PAYMENT

❏ Check enclosed (to the ABA)   Name _____

❏ Visa   ❏ MasterCard   ❏ American Express

_____
Account Number   Exp. Date   Signature

Firm _____

Address _____

City _____ State _____ Zip _____

Phone Number _____ E-Mail Address _____

Guarantee
If—for any reason—you are not satisfied with your purchase, you may return it within 30 days of receipt for a complete refund of the price of the book(s). No questions asked!

Mail: ABA Publication Orders, P.O. Box 10892, Chicago, Illinois 60610-0892
♦ Phone: 1-800-285-2221 ♦ FAX: 312-988-5568

E-Mail: abasvcctr@americanbar.org ♦ Internet: http://www.lawpractice.org/catalog

Are You in Your Element?

Tap into the Resources of the ABA Law Practice Management Section

ABA Law Practice Management Section Membership Benefits

The ABA Law Practice Management Section (LPM) is a professional membership organization of the American Bar Association that helps lawyers and other legal professionals with the business of practicing law. LPM focuses on providing information and resources in the core areas of marketing, management, technology, and finance through its award-winning magazine, teleconference series, Webzine, educational programs (CLE), Web site, and publishing division. For more than thirty years, LPM has established itself as a leader within the ABA and the profession-at-large by producing the world's largest legal technology conference (ABA TECHSHOW®) each year. In addition, LPM's publishing program is one of the largest in the ABA, with more than eighty-five titles in print.

In addition to significant book discounts, LPM Section membership offers these benefits:

ABA TECHSHOW

Membership includes a $100 discount to ABA TECHSHOW, the world's largest legal technology conference & expo!

Teleconference Series

Convenient, monthly CLE teleconferences on hot topics in marketing, management, technology and finance. Access educational opportunities from the comfort of your office chair — today's practical way to earn CLE credits!

Law Practice Magazine

Eight issues of our award-winning *Law Practice* magazine, full of insightful articles and practical tips on Marketing/Client Development, Practice Management, Legal Technology, and Finance.

Law Practice Today

LPM's unique Web-based magazine covers all the hot topics in law practice management today — identify current issues, face today's challenges, find solutions quickly. Visit www.lawpracticetoday.org.

Law Technology Today

LPM's newest Webzine focuses on legal technology issues in law practice management — covering a broad spectrum of the technology, tools, strategies and their implementation to help lawyers build a successful practice. Visit www.lawtechnologytoday.org.

LawPractice.news

Monthly news and information from the ABA Law Practice Management Section

Brings Section news, educational opportunities, book releases, and special offers to members via e-mail each month.

To learn more about the ABA Law Practice Management Section, visit www.lawpractice.org or call 1-800-285-2221.

ABA LAW PRACTICE MANAGEMENT SECTION

MARKETING • MANAGEMENT • TECHNOLOGY • FINANCE